W9-BRZ-938

COSMIC CONSTITUTIONAL THEORY

INALIENABLE RIGHTS SERIES

. . .

Kathleen M. Sullivan
STANLEY MORRISON PROFESSOR OF LAW
STANFORD LAW SCHOOL

J. Harvie Wilkinson III
JUDGE U.S. COURT OF APPEALS FOR THE
FOURTH CIRCUIT

Laurence H. Tribe
CARL M. LOEB UNIVERSITY PROFESSOR OF LAW
HARVARD LAW SCHOOL

Kenji Yoshino
CHIEF JUSTICE EARL WARREN PROFESSOR OF
CONSTITUTIONAL LAW
NEW YORK UNIVERSITY SCHOOL OF LAW

Mark V. Tushnet
WILLIAM NELSON CROMWELL PROFESSOR OF LAW
HARVARD LAW SCHOOL

GEOFFREY STONE AND OXFORD UNIVERSITY PRESS GRATEFULLY ACKNOWLEDGE THE INTEREST AND SUPPORT OF THE FOLLOWING ORGANIZATIONS IN THE INALIENABLE RIGHTS SERIES: THE ALA THE CHICAGO HUMANITIES FESTIVAL THE AMERICAN BAR ASSOCIATION THE NATIONAL CONSTITUTION CENTER THE NATIONAL ARCHIVES

Cosmic Constitutional Theory

. . .

WHY AMERICANS ARE LOSING THEIR

INALIENABLE RIGHT TO SELF-GOVERNANCE

J. Harvie Wilkinson III

OXFORD
UNIVERSITY PRESS

OXFORD
UNIVERSITY PRESS

Oxford University Press, Inc., publishes works that further
Oxford University's objective of excellence
in research, scholarship, and education.

Oxford   New York
Auckland   Cape Town   Dar es Salaam   Hong Kong   Karachi
Kuala Lumpur   Madrid   Melbourne   Mexico City   Nairobi
New Delhi   Shanghai   Taipei   Toronto

With offices in
Argentina   Austria   Brazil   Chile   Czech Republic   France   Greece
Guatemala   Hungary   Italy   Japan   Poland   Portugal   Singapore
South Korea   Switzerland   Thailand   Turkey   Ukraine   Vietnam

Copyright © 2012 by Oxford University Press, Inc.

Published by Oxford University Press, Inc.
198 Madison Avenue, New York, NY 10016

www.oup.com

Oxford is a registered trademark of Oxford University Press

Library of Congress Cataloging-in-Publication Data
Wilkinson, J. Harvie, 1944–
Cosmic constitutional theory : why Americans are losing their inalienable right
to self-governance / J. Harvie Wilkinson III.
p. cm   (Inalienable rights series)
Includes bibliographical references and index.
ISBN 978-0-19-984601-6 (hardback : alk. paper)
1. Constitutional law—United States—Philosophy.
2. Constitutional law—Political aspects—United States.
3. Constitutional law—United States—Interpretation and construction.
4. Self-determination, National—United States.   I. Title.
KF4552.W55 2012   342.73001—DC23   2011023280

1 3 5 7 9 8 6 4 2
Printed in the United States of America
on acid-free paper

To my law clerks
Past and present
Who have enriched my life beyond measure

Contents

· · ·

CONTENTS

Editor's Note

. . .

We hold these truths to be self-evident, that all men are created equal, that they are endowed by their Creator with certain unalienable Rights...

The Declaration of Independence

Over the past half century, scholars, judges, and lawyers have struggled to articulate and defend competing theories of constitutional interpretation. The quest has been to find some principled way to give concrete meaning to the open-ended provisions of the Constitution. Should judges search for "original meaning," should they be "pragmatic" or "minimalist," should they enforce the "living Constitution"? Should judges be restrained in their understanding and enforcement of the rights, liberties, and limitations set forth in the Constitution, or is restraint abdication? Without some principled theory of constitutional interpretation, should courts even be in the business of enforcing the guarantees of "equal protection of the laws" or "due process of law" or "the freedom of speech"?

The search for some principled, overarching approach to constitutional interpretation has dominated contemporary constitutional law, and it is therefore no surprise that J. Harvie Wilkinson's *Cosmic Constitutional Theory* is the third volume in this series to tackle this fundamental challenge. But unlike Goodwin Liu, Pamela Karlan, and Christopher Schroeder's *Keeping Faith with the Constitution* and David Strauss's *The Living Constitution*, both of which set forth general theories of constitutional interpretation, Judge Wilkinson's *Cosmic Constitutional Theory* argues that such theories—both on the right and on the left—are ultimately both pointless and downright harmful.

Although conceding that each of these theories has some intellectual merit, Wilkinson concludes that they all fail in the end to restrain courts from yielding to the temptations of unprincipled judicial activism. "What's needed," he argues, "is not yet another theory but an escape from theorizing." Scholars and judges who persist in pushing "theory-driven" results "have forgotten that wisdom lies simply in knowing the limits of one's knowledge, that good sense is more often displayed in collective and diverse settings than in a rarefied appellate atmosphere, and that the language, structure, and history of law serve best as mediums of restraint rather than excuses for intrusion."

In his call for a return to judicial restraint, Judge Wilkinson sharpens the debate and offers piercing critiques of all of the current theories. Anyone defending any of the existing theories of constitutional interpretation will have to take on his carefully stated and insightful objections.

Geoffrey R. Stone, June 2011

COSMIC CONSTITUTIONAL THEORY

Introduction

MODERN CONSTITUTIONAL LAW has fallen victim to cosmic constitutional theory. Over the last fifty years, we have witnessed the rise of theories that purport to unlock the mysteries of our founding document much as Freud proposed to lay bare all of human behavior and Einstein attempted to explain the universe. These theories have their value. They have imparted important insights. But they have fallen woefully short of providing the grand and unifying constitutional vision that their promoters have proclaimed.

Constitutional theory has been with us in some form since the Federalist Papers, but its explosion is a relatively recent phenomenon. Some of the theories originated in attempts to coordinate constitutional law with the novel rights that surfaced in the 1960s. Other theories then arose in reaction to that development and sought to stem the tide. Still other theories came about as an effort to mediate among the more absolute theoretical positions. And finally, yet more theories bubbled up as part of the ironic effort to stake out an antitheoretical position. Although an explosion of rights may initially have given rise to an explosion of theory, the theories have long since taken on a life of their own. No one has stepped back and asked exactly where these theoretical proliferations of all persuasions are taking us. The answer to that question will become clear: the theories are taking us down the road to judicial hegemony where the self-governance at the heart of our political order cannot thrive.

Indeed, the theories have given rise to nothing less than competing schools of liberal and conservative judicial activism, schools that have little in common other than a desire to seek theoretical cover for prescribed and often partisan results. In short, cosmic constitutional theory has done real damage to the rule of law, the role of courts in our society, and the ideals of restraint that the greatest judges in our country once embraced. But the worst damage of all has been to democracy itself, which theory has emboldened judges to displace.

What underlies this urge to come up with the theory of all theories? Perhaps it is the same impulse that led Sir Edmund Hillary to climb Mount Everest—one must scale the Constitution because it is there. Lofty aspirations are admirable, of course, so long as those who aspire to conquer the Constitution acknowledge that Sir Edmund just may have had the easier task.

This urge for unifying theory has its more practical aspect, in that constitutional interpretation is an instrument in the struggle for political power. The one who unlocks the secret of the constitutional atom will hugely influence how America shall be governed—defining not only the proper role for judges but the parameters of executive and legislative power, the place of the states in our system of dual sovereignty, and the balance between personal liberty and social order. Madison and Hamilton understood all too well the connection of constitutional theory to political power, as did Jackson and Calhoun, Lincoln and Douglas, Franklin Roosevelt and Ronald Reagan, to name but a few. The judges and academics who plumb the defining essence of the Constitution may seem more demure, but they too are keenly aware of the political stakes involved in gaining theoretical supremacy.

Then, too, a part of the urge to capture the Constitution must be purely personal. The document is tantalizing in its way, its riddles irresistible. But unlike the crossword, where one checks the answers, the constitutional puzzle is one the theorists can never know for sure they've solved. Alas, this may only add to the allure: "Bold Lover, never, never canst thou kiss, / Though winning near the goal…"[1]

If some cosmic theorist could capture the Constitution, it might be a real help to those of us in the trenches. We could set about our task of interpretation confident that we had the methodology correct and need only fret about the application. So the idea of helping out lesser legal mortals must play some part in the pursuit of cosmic theory. The gratitude to the theorist who finally gets it right, or most nearly so, would ensure that person's place in the pantheon. At the moment, however, we are left with many valuable insights from contemporary thinkers, but the one grand, unifying theory of the Constitution has yet to be found.

I make no pretense in this book of having a theory of my own with which to do the trick. I understand that to enter this vast terrain without a theory may strike some as traveling cross-country without a suitcase. Still, I am glad the search for cosmic theory has enlisted so many able participants. Whether it be the living constitutionalism of William Brennan, the originalism of Robert Bork, the political process theory of John Hart Ely, the textualism of Hugo Black, the minimalism of Cass Sunstein, the cost-benefit pragmatism of Richard Posner, the active liberty of Stephen Breyer, or the moral readings of Ronald Dworkin, the contribution of each must be respected. And even this is admittedly an arbitrary and far too abbreviated list. These estimable thinkers have two things in common. One is that they have enhanced our understanding of the world's most fascinating legal document and most powerful court. The other is that in their ultimate quest they have fallen very short.

Why has theory so failed us? Perhaps it is because the Constitution is not at bottom an abstraction. It is by nature less amenable to theory than to the experience that ground-level governance represents. Moreover, the Constitution was designed to resist answers and incorporate tensions rather than yield its secrets to a single or comprehensive viewpoint. The problem is that cosmic constitutional theories can falsely suggest simple answers to intractable problems, thereby abetting judicial hubris. The theories supply ingredients of appropriate constitutional interpretation, but only ingredients. To see them as answers is to succumb to the notion that a document as complex as the Constitution can somehow be bottled and pasteurized.

Some of the theories themselves have become finely spun, however, and I do not see their shortcomings primarily as ones of oversimplification. Rather, their failure stems from the fact that the attraction of constructing cosmic theory is itself too great. The temptation to go grand has blinded the theorists to humble thoughts. It has led to the subordination of the most basic and honorable of all judicial traditions, that republican virtue of judicial restraint. In some cases, the theorists have paid little more than lip service to the notion that judges should refrain from promoting their personal views of what is right and good. Living constitutionalists, for example, have other priorities than keeping the progressive instincts of the courts in check.

The more surprising development is that theories whose professed purpose was to constrain the courts have done anything but. And the hard and dispiriting reality is that such diverse doctrines as originalism, textualism, minimalism, pragmatism, and process theory, all propounded in varying degrees with a measure of restraint in mind, have at best failed in their announced purpose and at worse left restraint in an even more embattled state. The result has been to strip the courts of their mantle and to leave them in what is frankly a more nakedly political state.

Why is judicial restraint so important? One could give a complicated answer, but the simplest response is by all odds the best. Our system of governance gives judges both life tenure and virtually the last word on a document that is at once supremely important and maddeningly inexact. Because the normal constraints on the exercise of power are lacking, America places a big bet that judges will restrain themselves. But this bet goes against eons of human experience and would make Lord Acton, who recognized that "power tends to corrupt and absolute power corrupts absolutely," roll over in his grave. Realizing that placing bets on self-restraint is by all objective measures foolhardy is meant ideally to inspire the judiciary to return society's trust by placing limits on itself.

What are the consequences if we fail to do so? It is easy enough for us to uphold free speech when we agree with what is being said. It is easy enough for us to follow precedent when we like where it leads. It is easy enough to apply the plain language of statutes when we would have voted to enact them. And it is easy enough to uphold the constitutionality of a law of which we wholeheartedly approve. That is the easy part. But the test is whether we refrain from flattening the speech and precedent and laws which we deplore. If we flunk that test—if we fail to exercise restraint—then we forsake the rule of law, embody only our own preferences and prejudices, and deal the people and their democratic institutions a staggering blow.

Surely the leading thinkers in the law should have helped avert this signal danger to self-governance. But they have instead abetted it. It is this development that I wish to explore—the surprising inability of modern constitutional theories of all stripes to restrain courts from imposing on others their personal vision of the proper good. I do not expect judges to divest themselves of the essential quality of judgment or to shrink from unpopular rulings under law. But cosmic constitutional theory, for all its value, has simply provided inadequate incentives for judges to be judges. The result has been to deprive courts of their chief source of stature as the one branch of government distinct and apart from the ebb and flow of political life. Theories that ostensibly begin with different purposes and methods and nomenclature end with a similar absence of assurance that our robes display the dispassion that law at its most noble requires.

One may, of course, question the causal connection between cosmic theory and the justices who actually sit on the bench. It can, I suppose, be argued that the theorists inhabit one abstract and academic world, while judges handle the more practical, atheoretical task of actually deciding a case. It is true that the justices don't go around citing theorists. At least I have never known one of them to say "I'm following Ely" or "I'm following Bork."

But to pretend that the justices are unaware or uninfluenced by the seminal theoretical contributions of the last several decades seems to me naive. Surely they are not that isolated. The profession is not hermetically sealed in separate academic and judicial spheres. Discussion of the theorists is in fact pervasive. Living constitutionalism, originalism, and other theories to a lesser degree have permeated the consciousness of at least the educated public—if not in full refinement of detail, at least in blunt thrust.

The theories all have as their underpinning a far more active engagement in the affairs of democracy and the political branches than would any consistent commitment to restraint. To pretend they have no influence on the bench is to hold the untenable position that the world of ideas has wholly passed the judiciary by. One might still think that judges inclined to find their own political preferences in the Constitution can accomplish that goal without the assistance of theory. Indeed, some judges have. But in those instances where theory does not provide the rationale for politicized judging, it at least provides the cover, making the expedition into activism appear more respectable or more defensible than it otherwise would or should.

The great casualty of cosmic constitutional theory has been our inalienable right of self-governance. Well-intentioned though they may be, the theorists have blinded judges and scholars alike to this first principle of our constitutional order. Moreover, theory's siege on self-governance is hardly complete. Contemporary issues such as same-sex-marriage bans and health care reform have provoked a spate of constitutional challenges. The often understandable distaste of dedicated activists for measures such as Proposition 8's ban on same-sex marriages in California and the Patient Protection and Affordable Care Act has done little to assuage the larger fear that courts will use their own preferences to resolve our most volatile political controversies and that democratic liberty will once again be compromised.

It would be a mistake, however, to focus on the outcome of any single case as a barometer of the larger trend. As unfortunate as cosmic theory's contribution to the activism of the past has been, by far the greater danger lies ahead. For the ingredients of the cosmic theories are so stacked against self-governance that the temptations for judicial misadventures will only increase in years to come. And the admirable intellect and utmost sincerity displayed by leading theorists of all hues and stripes should only increase our consternation over the common danger they pose to democracy.

It will be noted that some of the most damaging blows against a theory are landed by other theorists. One might be tempted to remark that a gathering of constitutional theorists resembles nothing so much as a circular firing squad.[2] There are two reasons for this phenomenon. One is that the theorists are unusually adept at argument—at no time more so than when their own theories are under assault. The second reason has to do with their common vulnerability. The theorists are exposed to one another's depredations precisely because they have failed the threshold test—to show that the task of protecting constitutional liberty can be accomplished with respect for democratic institutions and the basic mandates of the given law.

I propose to scrutinize some of the leading constitutional theories to make my point. The labor is one of appreciation as much as criticism, even where the latter is pointed and sharp. The theorists make for fascinating reading, and their knowledge and understanding of constitutional governance runs deep. I shall attempt to credit their achievements, notwithstanding my conviction that the astonishing legal heights to which they aspire have inculcated immodesty in courts and made constitutional forbearance a lost and bygone art.

No theory of interpretation is or can be perfect. No theory can keep every headstrong impulse on the bench in check. Judges are human and hence flawed, and I am certain that I am as tempted by the prospect of congenial outcomes as the jurists to my right and to my left. But it is the job of modern constitutional theory to counteract, not reinforce, such tendencies, and in this it has not at all succeeded. "A persistently disturbing aspect of constitutional law is its lack of theory," Judge Robert Bork stated at the outset of his noted article on neutral principles and the First Amendment.[3] What is lacking, however, is not theory but the virtue of simple modesty that no longer beckons courts. The theorists have made modesty impossible, and it is our country's loss.

CHAPTER ONE

Living Constitutionalism: Activism Unleashed

THE "LIVING CONSTITUTION" is an evocatively flexible metaphor: it is "a coat of many colors,"[1] "a broad tent."[2] While the theory has many exponents, it is fair to begin this brief review with Justice William J. Brennan, who trumpeted this cosmic constitutional theory throughout a long career. Brennan overcame both family strains and financial difficulties to become a warm and influential presence on the Supreme Court.[3] A 1985 speech of Justice Brennan's expounds his theory of living constitutionalism unabashedly and leaves no doubt of his rejection of classical notions of restraint.[4]

Flush with laudable initial successes in curbing racial and gender discrimination and expanding the rights of free speech and to the assistance of counsel, Brennan and other living constitutionalists led the courts deep into the thickets of abortion, capital punishment, and habeas corpus. They endowed trial courts with broad authority over local school administration, extended the realm of constitutional tort at the expense of state and local governance, and were poised to confer broad constitutional protections on economic entitlements as well. In short, the influence of living constitutionalism has been exceeded only by the cumulative damage to democratic liberty that it inflicted.

A PRIMER ON LIVING CONSTITUTIONALISM

As we might expect a cosmic constitutional theory to do, Brennan's hermeneutical system boils down to a single question: "What do the words of the text mean in our time?"[5] Indeed, being up to date is the heart of Brennan's theory. First, Brennan believed that the evolution of textual meaning is not only possible but desirable. Second, he emphatically rejected original intent and original public meaning as the key to constitutional interpretation. Finally, Brennan acknowledged that living constitutionalism might pose a threat to self-governance by overturning the fruits of the majoritarian political process. To solve that problem, he encouraged judges to implement the contemporary values of the American people when the political process failed to take those values into account.

Brennan followed the tradition of the great common law realists in embracing the fact of constitutional evolution.[6] He considered this evolution of constitutional meaning to be "inevitable," even in the absence of textual amendments. For Brennan this evolution was not only inevitable but indeed a good of the highest order: "[T]he genius of the Constitution rests...in the adaptability of its great principles to cope with current problems and current needs." This adaptability was crucial to Brennan's fight to recognize and advance the principle of "human dignity," which was for him the supreme constitutional ideal.[7]

Much of constitutional interpretation has to do with time. What matters most—past intentions, present values, or future consequences? As to this, Brennan left little doubt where he stood. He flatly rejected the idea that either the original public meaning of the Constitution or the Framers' original understanding was sufficient for the resolution of all constitutional questions. Brennan considered such interpretation suited only for "a world that is dead and gone." With characteristic rhetorical force, he criticized the use of original intent as "arrogance cloaked as humility" because the relevant evidence is too "sparse or ambiguous" to support any reliable conclusions.[8] He therefore smelled hypocrisy when contemporary originalists advertised their approach as neutral, because reliance on original intent, along with its corresponding presumption against minority rights, "is a choice no less political than any other."[9]

Acknowledging the problem of placing the government's "coercive force" behind constitutional decisions that appear to "countermand the will of a contemporary majority," Brennan consistently located the key to democratic legitimacy not so much in the decisions of majorities long ago—as the originalists would have it—as in the implementation of contemporary American values in constitutional cases. It is "the community's interpretation"—one not invariably embodied in state and federal laws—"that is sought," rather than the Framers' expectations.[10] If, in this view, a constitutional decision can be framed as an implementation of a modern majority's understanding of a constitutional principle, then that decision is not an antidemocratic aberration but in fact a triumph of the will of the people.

THE VIRTUES OF LIVING CONSTITUTIONALISM

Whatever flaws his theory may have (and there are many), Justice Brennan was an intellectual force on the Court. The most obvious strength of living constitutionalism is its descriptive force: for better or for worse, it purports to describe where American constitutional law is and how it got there. The history of American constitutional law is, at least in part, the history of "precedents [that] evolve, shaped by notions of fairness and good policy" that inevitably reflect the modern milieu of the judges.[11] Even the attempts to apply other methodologies can bleed into living constitutionalism, because the recurring "tendency of judges to think that the law is what they would like it to be" will result in the projection of "current, modern values" onto critical cases.[12]

Promoting Stability in the Constitutional Corpus Juris

It is no surprise, then, that the landscape of modern American law is replete with living constitutionalist landmarks like an expansive congressional commerce power,[13] a broad role for regulatory agencies,[14] and a vibrant stable of unenumerated individual rights.[15] The dramatic presence of these constitutional fixtures has caused living constitutionalists to claim that their evolutionary theories, ironically, might promote the stability of the law as well. To the extent that other cosmic theories would require established doctrines to be cast out in part or en masse, they would upend the constitutional corpus juris. If a theory would require revisiting the most basic congressional powers, dismantling the administrative state, and overturning a whole host of rights on which citizens now rely, "isn't that a problem with the theory?"[16]

Thus have the reformers come to present themselves as stabilizers, perhaps in order to consolidate their gains. "The modern activist state," Brennan claimed, "is a concomitant of the complexity of modern society; it is inevitably with us."[17] The fact that some cases underpinning plenary enumerated powers, extensive regulatory reach, and expansive unenumerated rights might be of dubious soundness to begin with fails to answer the question of whether it is now advisable to overturn them. Do originalists really want to turn back the clock on matters of personal privacy? Do they really want to restore antiquated notions of inequality? For the originalists must at some point make their peace with the modern world and recent precedent, or risk irrelevancy.

Adherence to precedent is not merely a concession to the inevitability of evolution; it can be a powerful tool for judicial restraint in its own right. David Strauss, a living constitutionalist who finds a valuable role for precedential reasoning in constitutional adjudication, advises that a "judge who conscientiously tries to follow precedent is significantly limited in what she can do." Precedent serves as a leash not only because it provides "substantial guidance" in the form of cases and doctrines, but also because there are "fairly well developed standards" for evaluating judges engaged in the analysis of it.[18] That claim of course raises the question of whether living constitutionalists respected precedent in the first place. But to the extent that living constitutionalism now embraces the constraining force of stare decisis, it can be a force for judicial restraint.

In addition to reasoning by precedent, living constitutionalists often claim for themselves the virtue of incorporating the common law method generally in constitutional adjudication. This approach is advantageous, according to living constitutionalists, because of the desirable incrementalism and inherent adaptability of the common law approach. Living constitutionalists can sound very soothing when they wish to. Common law, they remind us, is by nature evolutionary, not revolutionary. Strauss identifies this incrementalism as the "common-sense notion" of traditionalism that holds "that any radical reexamination of existing ways of doing things is likely to discard good practices...and is unlikely to find very many better ones."[19] Strauss finds in the development of constitutional libel doctrine and free speech doctrine generally—hardly products of originalism or textualism—a shining example of this incremental method at work: "It developed over time, fitfully, by a process in which principles and standards were tried and sometimes eventually accepted, sometimes abandoned, sometimes modified, in light of experience and an ongoing, explicit assessment of whether they were sound as a matter of policy."[20]

Incrementalism also bears some kinship to adaptability. Brennan, echoing the common law giant Cardozo,[21] considered adaptability to "current problems and current needs" to be "the genius of the Constitution," a feature necessary to protect individual rights against a government reaching ever farther into "those areas of our lives once marked 'private.'"[22] We shall see shortly that this adaptability has indeed been an occasional virtue of living constitutionalism; the claimed incremental quality of living constitutionalism, however, has often been anything but.

The debate between living constitutionalists and originalists has become so polarized that it seems almost heresy to recognize that each theory has some merits. As I will show shortly, living constitutionalism is one of the most significant encouragements to freewheeling judging that has yet been devised. But to say that it has *no* validity or *no* merit in any situation is simply to overstate the indictment. Living constitutionalism is vulnerable on so many grounds that its opponents can surely afford to give it its due. And its due inheres in giving the elected branches leeway to craft fruitfully modern definitions of terms like "equality" and "commerce." With regard to equality, living constitutionalism has played an important part in adapting the Constitution itself, as well as alerting the elected branches to the need for moving on their own, toward the eradication of invidious discrimination in the United States. As to commerce, living constitutionalism has given a modern understanding to the forms of commerce that have developed in American life and has granted Congress the tools to deal with commercial developments that are both integrated and interstate.

Helping the Elected Branches Advance Equality

Living constitutionalism got the ball rolling in the elimination of overt discrimination on the basis of immutable characteristics—most importantly race. The most potent and enduring symbol of the Court's stand against such invidious discrimination was the declaration in *Brown v. Board of Education* that de jure segregation in public schools violates the equal protection of the laws.[23] It is not surprising that with the passage of time some have come to question the Supreme Court's seminal role in ending officially sanctioned segregation.[24] But those who were there at the time—black and white—knew all too well the entrenched nature of separatist practices and the political risks involved in challenging them. Whether *Brown* or *Marbury v. Madison* was the Court's most important decision may be debatable, but what cannot be disputed is that modern America's debt to the *Brown* Court is incalculable. Yet *Brown* was not and perhaps cannot be situated in the original understanding of the Constitution,[25] nor could it have been secured by formal amendment because the "immense effort by the people as a whole" that Article V requires most often makes textual amendments impossible.[26] *Brown* affords living constitutionalists a nonoriginalist case whose ultimate salutary effect on American equality properly renders the result nearly immune from criticism.[27]

Originalists in fact seem reluctant to recognize the full magnitude of living constitutionalism's contribution to the antidiscrimination principle. Though it certainly did not end de jure segregation overnight, *Brown* and its progeny did alert the elected branches of the need to move on their own, ultimately fashioning a fruitful partnership. Congress responded ten years after *Brown* with a forceful blow for racial equality in the form of the Civil Rights Act of 1964.[28] In fact, the elected branches succeeded far more in attacking invidious racial discrimination than the Court had on its own.[29] The Court was instrumental, however, in guaranteeing that the Civil Rights Act would not go unenforced.[30] The Court also participated with the elected branches in the campaign to address discrimination against women,[31] a campaign which gained momentum after *Brown* and the 1964 Civil Rights Act.[32] The transition from combating intentional discrimination to challenging disparate effects and from racial discrimination to discrimination on the basis of gender or sexual orientation presented much trickier questions than the *Brown* Court confronted. None of this is to deny, however, that rank discrimination against historically disadvantaged groups was a blight upon this country that living constitutionalism did well to alleviate.

Allowing Congress to Regulate Contemporary Commerce

By allowing the legislative branch to update constitutional terms like "commerce," living constitutionalism also made contributions to democratic accountability, legislative flexibility, and judicial restraint that originalist interpretation would not allow. Before the ascendancy of the living constitutionalist commerce clause, Congress was hamstrung by the Court's refusal to allow it to address issues that had become national in scope. The Court intervened early—refusing to apply antitrust regulations to a manufacturing monopoly in 1895[33]—and often, overturning New Deal legislation well into the Great Depression.[34] It was the living constitutionalist approach—not originalism—that permitted the judiciary both to show a measure of restraint and to allow Congress the flexibility to update the meaning of "commerce" as national exigency demanded.[35]

It could hardly have been otherwise. Activity that was properly deemed local and noncommercial in the separate enclaves of eighteenth-century life is now frequently swept into "the single, national market" through new means of transportation and communication, new methods of marketing, and advances in productivity and the like.[36] This is particularly apparent when the effects of that activity are viewed in aggregation rather than atomistically.[37] And the danger to national economic health now lies not only in arming Congress with an unlimited commerce power but also in arming courts with the authority to strike down congressional enactments through the disconcertingly subjective notion that the regulated activity lacks "substantial" economic effects.[38] That one may now fairly debate whether the modern commerce power is *too* open ended is a testament to the success of the living constitutionalist effort.[39] Only after the Court accorded Congress the freedom to act could meaningful democratic accountability attach to Congress's attempts to address the challenges of America's increasingly integrated and interstate commercial realm.

In its willingness to allow the political branches to pursue more modern conceptions of equality and commerce, living constitutionalism has made no small contribution and has in fact been more of a restraining force on judges than originalism. There is, however, a world of difference between courts allowing the elected branches to address contemporary problems and judges undertaking to do so on their own. It is living constitutionalism's willingness to blur this distinction that is among its large infirmities.

THE VICES OF LIVING CONSTITUTIONALISM

Whatever the virtues of living constitutionalism may be, judicial restraint is not among them. Perhaps more than any other cosmic constitutional theory, living constitutionalism, both in theory and in practice, has elevated judicial hubris over humility, boldness over modesty, and intervention over restraint.

Disrespecting the Democratic Will

To begin with, the theory at heart is "anti-democratic."[40] Whether the goal is positive entitlements[41] or substantive rights to privacy,[42] living constitutionalism charges judges with the task of creating a better world. This call to judicial supremacy is unfortunately replete with vague exhortations about "human dignity,"[43] "evolving standards of decency,"[44] and the perceived demands of justice and needs of society. And even when the prescriptions are not wrapped in pious language, they often reflect, as in the Court's school busing decisions, the notion that large-scale dislocations could be imposed upon parents and children by a single federal judge in pursuit of proportionate school enrollments that may or may not have advanced the educational achievements of the students affected.[45] In the process, living constitutionalism comes perilously close to abandoning the posture of restraint that makes judicial authority acceptable in the first place. The originalists who served as Brennan's principal sparring partners charged that law created by judges under the guise of living constitutionalism lacked formal democratic legitimacy. Justice Rehnquist put it nicely:

> To the extent that it makes possible an individual's persuading one or more appointed federal judges to impose on other individuals a rule of conduct that the popularly elected branches of government would not have enacted and the voters have not and would not have embodied in the Constitution,...the living Constitution is genuinely corrosive of the fundamental values of our democratic society.[46]

To make matters worse, the fruits of living constitutionalism that are produced outside of proper democratic channels cannot even be repaired inside those channels.[47] In short, living constitutionalism is a complete inversion of democratic primacy and turns the Constitution's foremost premise of popular governance on its head.

Of course, pure democracy is far from perfect. It can be consumed by gridlock. It can fasten on short-term partisan advantage, while long-term national problems fester. As the debt ceiling debates of 2011 showed, democracy can make one want to rise in the morning and shout "good riddance." Democracy can exhibit the failings of intolerance, bias, ignorance, venality, panic, capture, corruption, and other ills, some of which the Constitution rather explicitly gives the judiciary the authority to check. For some living constitutionalists, "unconstrained, vulgar democracy...may have many virtues, but it has many more flaws," flaws which are said to necessitate expanded judicial oversight.[48] But this emphasis on the shortcomings of democratic governance slights its virtues and ignores an inescapable truth. The imperfections of democracy are the imperfections of the human condition, which, by the way, have not passed the judicial branch by. And the messiness of democracy is often little more than government in action, with all its attendant disputatiousness and untidy compromises.

The problems addressed by democratic institutions are sometimes so large—war and peace, the scope and size of government—that no one should suppose the solutions will be pretty or simple. Yet that is no reason for judges to charge in. It is all too easy for those accustomed to the ordered solemnity of courts to regard the cruder discourse of politicians with disdain. And yet we judges are not general arbiters of majoritarian dysfunction. That task is most often left to other checks and balances—to the clashes of Congress and the executive, to the back-and-forth of bicameral legislatures, to the tug-of-war between state and federal governments, and ultimately, through a never-ending cycle of elections, to the people themselves. Living constitutionalism by contrast envisions the courts as intervenors du jour rather than a branch of government dedicated to the proposition that even a democracy that takes "wrong turns" must be allowed a decent latitude to play itself out.

For all their drawbacks, democratic institutions are still ours in a way that courts are not.

Ignoring Institutional Limitations

The fact is that judges are not suited for the robust role that living constitutionalists envision for them. Suppose that living constitutionalists are correct in their claim that the Constitution permits—indeed, commands—evolutionary "updating" of the Constitution in accordance with contemporary values. The question still remains who the updating agents should be. Brennan's living constitutionalism asserts a powerful, perhaps exclusive role for *judges* in this updating process.[49]

But the Constitution is not the courts' exclusive property. It belongs in fact to all three branches and ultimately to the people themselves.[50] America would be a much impoverished country if the political branches and the states surrendered all constitutional discourse to the courts, yet that is exactly what living constitutionalism has encouraged them to do. Judicial review may give courts the final constitutional word. But it does not give them the *only* word, and this recognition should make the ultimate exercise of invalidating popular enactments both a sparing and a sober one.

In the absence of defects in the political process, it is desirable for legislatures, rather than courts, to update social norms. First of all, courts are less adept than legislatures at assessing the precise content of society's values. Second, courts are less adroit than political institutions in assessing and reacting to changed circumstances. Finally, judicial updating can itself stunt the development of processes that are natural, nourishing, and necessary for the democratic spirit. Therefore, living constitutionalism, at least in its Brennanite incarnation, suffers from the vice of institutional blindness that all too commonly afflicts judicial activism.

If judges are to be the living constitution's modernizers, we ought at least to ask whether they will be any good at it. After all, the virtue of restraint lies in the recognition of one's own limitations. And the limitations of the judiciary are considerable. Legislators—at least those who hope to be reelected—must actually meet their constituents, understand their concerns, and press for their interests in the legislature. Federal appellate judges—whose job security surpasses even that of the most ensconced incumbent—spend the vast majority of their time in the monastic environment of chambers with only a minuscule staff. Sustained contact with the public is difficult, and discussion with members of the public most interested in a judge's ruling can be a grave breach of ethics. Most judges are sociable enough, but compared to legislative service, ours is an introverted calling. With regard to the capacity for comprehending "the nation's best understanding of its fundamental values,"[51] the comparison between legislator and judge is, in the vast majority of cases, no comparison at all.

It is not only what the legislator does but who the legislator is that makes the legislature the superior updater. The fact that a value is "fundamental" or claimed to stem from a vague and cryptic constitutional provision does not somehow render it unfathomable to representative government. The multitude and relative diversity of representative institutions makes them more likely than courts to accurately assess the content of the fundamental values of America as a whole.[52] Indeed, Congress was structured precisely to ensure the broad representation of the American people.[53] This representation is not only broad—it is constantly updated by the elections that take place, for example, every two years in the House of Representatives. "Courts," however, "are not representative bodies. They are not designed to be a good reflex of a democratic society."[54] Nothing in the Constitution suggests that councils composed exclusively of lawyers were meant to be America's reigning class. For all these reasons, appellate judges must recognize the danger that James Wilson identified early in the republic: "With regard to the sentiments of the people," it is "difficult to know precisely what they are. Those of the particular circle in which one move[s] [are] commonly mistaken for the general voice."[55]

The dangers of judges operating at a far remove from representative government are nowhere as evident as in that exemplar of evolutionary constitutionalism: the Eighth Amendment's prohibition on cruel and unusual punishment. In 2011, the Supreme Court somehow thought that this provision justified the release of some 46,000 inmates from the California state prison system due to what the five-member majority viewed as "systemic" unconstitutional conditions of confinement.[56] There is a big difference, however, between a general recognition that some prison conditions are substandard and taking upon oneself the authority to make profoundly consequential tradeoffs between penal environments and public safety. Only judges persuaded that the Living Constitution empowers them to strike quintessentially legislative balances for the states would have adopted so rash a remedy as mass release, a remedy hardly compelled by the Prison Litigation Reform Act or indeed by any act of Congress. Justice Alito in dissent not surprisingly warned that the Court's "premature release of approximately 46,000 *criminals—the equivalent of three Army divisions*" would be "very likely to have a major and deleterious effect on public safety,"[57] a fact most unlikely to be overlooked in a legislative setting.

A second reason to be skeptical of judges as constitutional updaters is that even if judges accurately gauge the constitutional mood at any given time, they will be hard pressed to remove newly fashioned substantive rights from the constitutional roster when that mood shifts. To be honest, the judicial system, for all its virtues, is not always eager to admit its mistakes. Judges must be convinced their prior views were wrong. And, of course, the judge as guardian of the evolving Constitution must be persuaded that someone else's constitutional wisdom has now been proven superior to his own. To say that human nature resists the retraction of rights already afforded is an understatement; this barrier is hardly removed by the maxim that "claims of *stare decisis* are at their weakest" in constitutional decisions.[58]

Brennan's own example poignantly illustrates judicial failure to adjust constitutional values in both directions in accordance with the public will. After concurring in *Furman v. Georgia*, which imposed a de facto moratorium on capital punishment in the mid-1970s, Justice Brennan dissented in *Gregg v. Georgia*,[59] in which a majority of the Court voted to end the moratorium. He continued to dissent thereafter on the grounds that the death penalty is per se "cruel and unusual punishment."[60] Though Brennan acknowledged that his decision in *Furman* depended on drawing meaning from "evolving standards of decency,"[61] he refused to acquiesce in the evolving judgment, reflected in the legislatures of at least thirty-five states, that the death penalty did not offend the most up-to-date standards.[62] Brennan's refusal was all the more pointed because he admitted that his view did not reflect the nation's contemporary values.[63] If this view is at all characteristic of living constitutionalists, then judicial updating of the Constitution is problematic, because it will tend to create a one-way ratchet that the people can do little to turn back.

The final reason that it is preferable to have the legislature be the one to update is that judicial updating can strangle democratic vigor. One foundational premise of the American experiment is that self-determination is a valuable good. Popular participation in government creates a whole host of benefits that arise

> from the vigorous thinking that ha[s] to be done in the political debates…, from the infiltration through every part of the population

of sound ideas and sentiments, from the rousing into activity of opposite elements, the enlargement of ideas, the strengthening of moral fibre, and the growth of political experience.

Indeed, even when the fruits of that participation are flawed, there is often great value in "the political experience, and the moral education and stimulus that come from fighting the question out in the ordinary way."[64]

By contrast, when *judges* take it upon themselves to update the Constitution in the name of the popular will, they deprive "all participants, even the losers, the satisfaction of a fair hearing and an honest fight."[65] When a court declares certain rights or powers beyond the legislative capacity, Americans can no longer attempt to persuade their fellow citizens on these issues in the legislative arena and can no longer enjoy the intellectual and psychic satisfactions of reasoned republican self-rule. This point should not be taken too far—of course some values are sufficiently fundamental to be beyond the reach of legislative deliberation, but they are ordinarily limited to those explicitly mentioned in our founding document.[66] But activism of the vague and unenumerated varieties sanctioned by living constitutionalism eventually stunts the natural capacities and faculties of citizens; restraint by encouraging self-governance enlarges them. Even if judges weren't already ineffective at updating the Constitution, this impairment of the democratic exercise would be a compelling reason to leave legislatures as the primary updaters of society's basic beliefs.

Overlooking Textual Constraints

If the institutional limitations of living constitutionalism weren't bad enough, then its reliance on judges to draw specific direction from the Constitution's most general formulations renders judicial restraint practically impossible. Living constitutionalists argue that the document's generality implies a certain style of jurisprudence—that the Framers composed constitutional guarantees in spacious terms in order to afford judges a degree of interpretive latitude to apply those guarantees to contemporary situations. This overlooks the fact, however, that the Framers may have had many motivations, rhetorical and otherwise, for general expression besides empowering the judiciary. Indeed, relatively little elsewhere in the document indicates that an ever-increasing displacement of democracy was in order. In fact, the spacious language should be interpreted as a yellow light to courts, rather than a green one, an injunction to judges not to apply the Constitution's vaguest provisions to subjects that all the evidence indicates the Framers never had in mind.

The danger, of course, is that for living constitutionalists willing to accept the sufficiency of the most attenuated relationship between a decision and the textual, structural, and historical methods that should guide it, the capacious language of the constitutional vessel simply provides too much temptation for judges to pour their own beliefs in. For judges constrained by so little, the attraction must be so great. Consider the doctrine of substantive due process, which allows judges to create *substantive* rights from the Fourteenth Amendment's guarantee of due *process*, rights which the Amendment never mentioned and which the legislature by definition cannot touch. Despite the failure of this doctrine to keep earlier judges from enacting their own views into constitutional law,[67] it was enthusiastically embraced by Brennan and his contemporaries, to similar effect.[68] It is true that the Supreme Court's substantive due process interventions in the early decades of the twentieth century involved primarily the invalidation of economic regulation of asserted business prerogatives,[69] while interventions in later decades largely struck down laws invading rights of personal privacy and autonomy. Though scholars have debated the relative persuasiveness of the different rationales for activism, the fact remains that presidents as different as Franklin Roosevelt and Ronald Reagan expressed intense public displeasure with the Court's aggressive Fourteenth Amendment course.

That the transition from one flawed substantive due process era to another occurred without evident irony or embarrassment is remarkable. *Roe v. Wade*, the marquee substantive due process decision of the latter era, flunked simultaneously the three most basic interpretive tests. Nothing in the text of the Constitution suggested that the specific contours of a right to abortion should be judicially engrafted onto a highly generalized privacy right. Nothing in the structure of the Constitution indicated that judges were to substitute their own will on the question for that of the states and the elected branches. And nothing in the history of the Fourteenth Amendment suggested that its framers had abortion or anything like it on their minds. After its failing marks on accepted interpretive methods, the question was of course raised: what constraints, if any, is living constitutionalism prepared to recognize?

All too few it seems. The apparent absence of constraint in living constitutionalism was by no means limited to its innovations in substantive due process. It is often overlooked that the boldest putsch attempted by living constitutionalists was actually in the realm of economic entitlements, which were deemed at least by earlier generations of living constitutionalists to be fundamental rights. In the early 1970s, living constitutionalists launched an audacious project in which the judiciary itself was to provide a constitutional guarantee for the terms of subsistence and opportunity in the modern age. For example, Justice Marshall, dissenting in *Dandridge v. Williams* with Justice Brennan, sought to apply rigorous scrutiny to a state's decision to limit welfare grants and to invigorate "the Equal Protection Clause as a constitutional principle applicable to the area of social welfare administration."[70] Likewise in *Lindsey v.*

Normet[71] and *San Antonio Independent School District v. Rodriguez*,[72] the dissenters expressed a willingness to craft judicial entitlements to housing and public education, respectively.

The upshot of this development would have been to make the judiciary a coequal partner with the legislative and executive branches in large areas of domestic policy. The constitutionalization of public assistance, for instance, would have given the judicial branch a role in policing the adequacy of appropriations for welfare payments under who knows what criteria. This injudicious attempt to create judicial entitlements was repulsed by the good sense of other justices, who understood that the basic nature of the Constitution was to operate as a negative prohibition upon certain government intrusions and not as a fountain of positive rights.[73] But the attempted transformation of our charter remains one of the most dangerous constitutional bullets that America has ever dodged, and those who witnessed this near miss could be forgiven for hoping that something like the constraint of originalism would provide a necessary antidote for warding off future eras of judicial excess.

If the constraints of text, structure, and history have no purchase on living constitutionalists, what does? The much-ballyhooed constraint of precedent did not serve that function in the *Roe* decision, because little in the circumscribed contraception precedents of *Griswold* and *Eisenstadt* suggested the tectonic shift to an abortion right in *Roe*. And while living constitutionalists often point to the incrementalism and adaptability of the common law method as tools of constraint,[74] the great common law judges did not purport to be handling publicly enacted law. In any event, the legislative branch was always free to overrule their common law decisions. In the hands of common law judges, common law methods were indeed a constraint; in the hands of the living constitutionalists in *Roe* or, for that matter, the dissenters in *Dandridge* and *Rodriguez*, common law modesty and incrementalism were cast aside. All that remained was living constitutionalism, claiming for itself the bold and final word.

So yet again, the question arises: what exactly are the constraints on living constitutionalism? David Strauss, who trumpets the constraints of the common law method, finds that moral "judgments of fairness and policy are appropriate" whenever text and precedent are "weak, equivocal, or unsettled."[75] But what minimally inventive judge is unable to massage text and precedent to reach what he thinks is "a morally acceptable conclusion"?[76] Justice Souter asserts that judges are confined to the space between conflicting constitutional norms: "Judges have to choose between the good things that the Constitution approves, ... to value liberty, as well as order, and fairness and equality, as well as liberty."[77] Ronald Dworkin claims that abstract "moral principles about political decency and justice" must guide judges,[78] but, like Justice Souter, cannot give a satisfying answer to such questions as: whose morality? whose decency? whose fairness? whose justice? Such things are in the eye of the beholder, and the very reason we have a democracy is that on many sensitive questions, views of fairness, morality, and justice might legitimately diverge.

There is often no one right resolution to the most vexing moral, social, and political issues roiling our society. The very existence of the multiple elective forums established by the Constitution presupposes that allowing different answers to some of our most disputatious questions is not at all a bad way to proceed. The vulnerability of living constitutionalism is that it appears ill suited to a pluralistic nation. The theory draws instead from narrow premises, reflecting elite segments of opinion derived from one profession only, selected eras of recent history (e.g., the 1960s), and the predominant views of an urban and coastal intelligentsia whose influence upon the intellectual processes of the judiciary appears to leave many ordinary Americans in the cold. The irony is that narrow opinions of elites often seem broad minded to those who hold them. Be that as it may, "claims that are inseparable from the customs that prevail in a certain region, the idiosyncratic expectations of a certain group, or the personal preferences of their champions, may be valid claims in some sense; but they are not of constitutional stature."[79] Restraint allows those whom the judicial process would exclude to be included in decisions. Though no political process and certainly no constitutional approach can succeed in making the voice of each citizen an equal one, at least restraint does not a priori shut such large segments of the American people out.

It is a stinging indictment of living constitutionalism that the ranks of its disciples on the bench have become so thin. The theory has proven a bit much for even the more liberal members of the present Court. Justice Stephen Breyer, for example, though he has embraced unenumerated substantive due process rights,[80] has not signed off on an absolutist view of the death penalty or positive economic entitlements—two of the most regrettable tenets of the earlier living constitutionalist view. Moreover, he has taken seriously the obligations of restraint in varied contexts, including congressional regulation of interstate commerce,[81] public displays with religious significance,[82] and firearms regulation,[83] to name but a few. The Justice is not always an exemplary practitioner of judicial restraint, but unlike Justices Brennan and Marshall, he does acknowledge the value of restraint and the compelling need for humility in judging.[84] That Breyer and his like-minded peers have rejected the more freewheeling variants of living constitutionalism is a cautionary note to those who would have the justices adopt this cosmic constitutional theory.

Living constitutionalism still has its legions of adherents, however, not all of whom are liberal. Indeed, in an odd twist of fate, the lineal descendants of living constitutionalism now include those Tea Party and economic libertarians who would find takings of property in broad swaths of local zoning regulations and who would use the contracts, just compensation, or due process clauses to disable Congress from setting such things as minimum wages under the Fair Labor Standards Act.[85] The fact that freewheeling constitutionalism may have come full circle and returned in part to its Lochnerian economic roots would no doubt cause Brennan to blanche. Such, alas, are the fruits of embracing a fickle creed of constitutional revisionism and setting aside a principled commitment to restraint.

So the theory lives on, with its imperishable allure for judges who would embrace their own higher values as a constitutional guide. In fairness, let us note that Justice Brennan was not entirely unconcerned with judicial restraint. He located the bounds of restraint not so much in the substance of his constitutional theory but rather in the institutional procedures of the judiciary itself: "the recording of precedent, and the requirement of a public and reasoned explanation of the judicial result."[86] Resting, perhaps, on the belief that these institutionalized sources of restraint largely account for whatever quantum of modesty is due, living constitutionalism has become a testament to the dangers of third-branch overreach. Brennan and his followers, in their quest for a constitution of evolving decency, neglected the fact that the people and their representatives also evolve and that their views on volatile questions, though disputable, are not on that account indecent. In its pure form, living constitutionalism is paternalism, premised on the belief that very few know what is best for very many, which is to say us all.

CHAPTER TWO

Originalism: Activism Masquerading as Restraint

JUDGE ROBERT BORK believed that constitutional theory could legitimize judicial review by constraining judges with neutral principles. A serious scholar and immensely decent man, Bork immersed himself in American constitutional history and political thought. Tantalized by the prospect of finding a theory with the power to unlock the secrets of the Constitution, Bork devoted much of his life to this quest. His efforts culminated in *The Tempting of America*, Bork's most complete statement and defense of his theory of originalism.[1] Originalism, with its myriad virtues, has an important role to play in constitutional adjudication, but it suffers from that all-too-common infirmity of cosmic constitutional theory: a lack of judicial restraint. In the case of originalism, this failing assumes almost a tragic dimension, because more than any other theory, it tried so earnestly and so hard to be an exemplar of the modest virtues.

THE ORIGINAL ORIGINALISTS

Originalism has been around, in one form or another, since the first days of the Constitution. Indeed, Chief Justice John Marshall routinely displayed originalist tendencies, considering the intentions of the Framers on all manner of topics, from the Fifth Amendment's applicability to the states,[2] to patent law,[3] to the Court's jurisdiction over conflicts between a state and Indian tribes in that state,[4] to the scope and meaning of the commerce clause,[5] to the Court's power to review state court decisions dealing with federal constitutional questions.[6] Likewise, Marshall factored what "the framers of the constitution contemplated" into his famous opinion in *Marbury v. Madison.*[7]

In the modern era, however, the justice who started originalism on its ascent to prominence was none other than Hugo Black. In some ways, this observation may seem counterintuitive, insofar as Black is widely considered to be more of a textualist than an originalist.[8] But in Black's view, the text was the best guide to what the Framers actually had in mind. This has led Professor Noah Feldman to claim that Black "was the first justice to frame originalism as a definitive constitutional theory and to explain why and how he was using it. In this sense, Black was the inventor of originalism."[9]

As a justice, Black had a marked righteous streak and was given to rather stark pronouncements. For Black, the font of interpretation was nothing more—or less—than the actual words of the Constitution. While Black did on occasion consider constitutional history and original intentions in determining his positions,[10] he generally took the more scriptural view that the Constitution's actual words and text sufficed for proper constitutional analysis.[11] *Griswold v. Connecticut* is illustrative of these views; while Black agreed with the majority that Connecticut's ban on the use of contraceptives in the marital bedroom was "offensive," he found himself unable to declare it unconstitutional because the text of the Constitution mentioned no right to privacy.[12] Other, more anecdotal evidence of Black's commitment to text abounds. In First Amendment cases, Black would apparently "walk around his office reciting a catechism to himself: 'What does the Constitution say?'...If the doctrine did not match the text, then the doctrine must be wrong."[13] Similarly, Black would routinely carry around a copy of the Constitution in his pocket to illustrate his commitment to the primacy of its text.[14]

Black's portable Constitution was more than just an idle gesture. His career plainly increased the devotion of Americans to their founding document and elevated the centrality of text in legal interpretations of all sorts. Although considered a liberal justice for much of his career, Black certainly tried to make textualism sound like a theory of restraint. He steadfastly rejected any school of interpretation that would render the "Court's members a day-to-day constitutional convention."[15] He sought to discourage judges from exploring the "limitless area of their own beliefs" to "actually select policies."[16] And he recognized that judges who indulge such impulses improperly arrogate the "power to make laws" in lieu of exercising their constitutionally guaranteed "power to interpret them."[17] Bork would later echo almost all of these sentiments.[18]

But in practice, Black's pure textualism ultimately came up short. Even the absolute textual command that "Congress shall make no law...abridging the freedom of speech"[19] raised questions about the protection of expressive conduct[20] and associative rights.[21] And that was only the beginning of the problem. It is of course true that text can limit judges; the Constitution has much to say on some topics and nothing to say on others. In these instances, even constitutional silences can be said to be instructive. But it is equally undeniable that many constitutional provisions are "extremely open-textured."[22] While the due process clause of the Fourteenth Amendment says that process is required, it does not say how much.

The equal protection clause mandates equal treatment under law but provides no specific definition of equality. And the privileges or immunities clause says that its namesakes may not be denied but leaves their definition open. Such boundless phrases invite an equally boundless interpretive discretion.

So a text that raises questions more than it provides answers can hardly be the linchpin of any theory of restraint. After all, a judge looking at nothing other than text will have ample opportunity to pour his or her own values into the Constitution. Just as a judge so inclined could ride the word "equal" far in the direction of a redistributionist state,[23] so too could a judge ride the word "contract" over many forms of social welfare legislation.[24] In other words, it can be just as activist to pretend that the Constitution's words provide all the answers as it is to ignore its text in order to reach outcomes one happens to approve.

Well before the end of Black's career, it became clear that his rudimentary textual originalism badly needed shoring up. Bork himself recognized the flaws in Black's approach. In *The Tempting of America*, he condemned the so-called Black-Douglas wing of the Supreme Court as exemplifying a result-oriented approach of "disguised activism."[25] Recognizing that text alone could not provide all the answers,[26] Bork began his search for a method of constitutional interpretation from a different starting point.

A PRIMER ON ORIGINALISM

Bork's search for a theory began with the Madisonian dilemma. The Constitution establishes a government around two principles that necessarily exist in tension: majority power and minority freedom. The Framers' genius lay in recognizing that "neither majorities nor minorities can be trusted to define the proper spheres of democratic authority and individual liberty." There are dangers at either extreme. Tyranny is tyranny, be it of the majority or the minority. The Framers balanced the competing principles of majority rule and minority freedom both structurally, by limiting the reach of and dispersing power within the national government, and substantively, through the Bill of Rights.[27]

The task of maintaining the balance between majority rule and minority rights falls to the courts. And it is from this duty that the need for constitutional theory arises. As Bork explains, constitutional theory must "define[] the spheres of the majority and the individual in a sense that can be called 'correct.'" By limiting the range of "correct" outcomes and providing a principled basis for rulings, constitutional theory checks the power of the judiciary and prevents rule by judicial fiat.[28]

But not just any theory will do. Bork turned to Professor Herbert Wechsler for guidance on the proper criteria.[29] As Wechsler explained, only a theory based on neutral principles will prevent the Supreme Court from becoming a "naked power organ."[30] Wechsler's insight was that justices must decide cases on the basis of principles that they are willing to apply neutrally, regardless of their personal preferences. Neutral application of principles provides a bulwark against political judging. But a crafty judge could derive and define these principles in a politically motivated manner, resulting in political decisions despite neutral application. Thus Bork contended that the only way to ensure that the Madisonian dilemma is resolved in a principled manner, instead of according to the political preferences of the justices, is to find a constitutional theory "capable of supplying neutrality in all three respects—in deriving, defining, and applying principle."[31]

Bork found only one theory capable of such triplicate neutrality: originalism. Originalism is neutral in deriving principles because it accepts the original public understanding of the Constitution as the only legitimate source of constitutional interpretation. It is the founding generation, not the contemporary judge, who strikes the balance between majority rule and minority freedom. Originalism is neutral in defining principles because principles derived from the Constitution can only be defined "at the level of generality that the text and historical evidence warrant." Originalism is neutral in applying principles because it directs judges to apply their neutrally derived and defined principles consistently, regardless of whether the outcome in a particular case might offend their own political preferences.[32]

In Bork's view, the original public understanding is the touchstone of constitutional analysis: "All that counts is how the words used in the Constitution would have been understood at the time." The subjective intentions of the drafters are of no moment. Secret intentions count for nothing in legal interpretation, and it should be no different for the Constitution. Of course, Bork does not claim that records of the convention debates or personal correspondence between the drafters are irrelevant. Far from it—the original public understanding is "manifested in the words used and in the secondary materials, such as debates at the conventions, public discussion, newspaper articles, dictionaries in use at the time, and the like."[33]

Bork treats the Constitution as a source of law to be interpreted and applied as such. The original public understanding provides a major premise, a value the Framers intended to protect. The judge must then supply the minor premise, determining whether this value is threatened by the subject matter of the case at hand. The conclusion follows. According to Bork, this process is the essence of the judicial craft. Judges apply this same analytical framework to statutes, precedents, and other sources of law.[34]

After reaching the correct result under the original understanding, a judge must next confront the question of precedent.

Under Bork's originalism, correct constitutional interpretation yields to precedent only if the previous decision has "become so embedded in the life of the nation, so accepted by the society, so fundamental to the private and public expectations of individuals and institutions, that the result should not be changed now." "Judging is not mechanical," and this determination relies heavily on judicial prudence.[35]

Originalism admittedly "requires a fair degree of sophistication and self-consciousness on the part of the judge."[36] And although originalist judges may err occasionally, Bork believes that originalism at the very least ensures that "judges will confine themselves to the principles the Framers put into the Constitution."[37] As for the most important question—whether originalism provides enough neutral guidance for judicial review to be legitimate under the Constitution—Bork was convinced that it does.[38]

THE VIRTUES OF ORIGINALISM

Originalism, though not without real flaws, has much to offer. It has rightfully earned its place among the pantheon of constitutional theories. The virtues of originalism are real, and they should not be cast aside because the theory is ultimately wanting. These virtues include providing judicial constraints; harnessing the judiciary's expertise in traditional legal analysis; offering a coherent justification for the judiciary's democratic legitimacy; and enjoying, at least on a basic level, a good measure of acceptance. Although it is perhaps an unintended byproduct of the doctrine, originalism has helped to rekindle interest in the nation's founding period. Even a modest reduction of historical illiteracy is no small achievement. Originalism deserves real credit for this contribution, even if it is not strictly a legal one.

Acknowledging the Importance of Constraint

Perhaps more than any other theory, originalism focuses on judicial constraints. Bork sought a theory capable of constraining judges through the use of neutral principles, thus providing a way for the judiciary to "check itself" and prevent the aggrandizement of its own power at the expense of the other branches.[39] This constraining focus of originalism is the basis of its appeal, accounting for "the prominence it has achieved in the last few decades as both a justification for and an objective constraint on the power of judicial review."[40] And, though it ultimately falls short, there is no denying that originalism has done much to popularize the notion that judges must indeed be constrained.

Of course, some constitutional provisions would constrain originalists and nonoriginalists alike. While lawyers can quibble over the meaning of just about anything, everyone agrees that the president must be at least thirty-five years old.[41] No one doubts that Congress has the power to establish a postal service.[42] But there are other issues where originalism provides clear answers and some nonoriginalist theories do not. For example, originalism resolves the question of whether there is a constitutional right to assisted suicide with a resounding no. As Chief Justice Rehnquist's opinion in *Washington v. Glucksberg* emphasizes, America's history from the founding era to the present is replete with punitive measures designed to curb suicide, and thus no originalist can claim that the original meaning of any constitutional provision grants this sort of right.[43] If this result seems too obvious to be of much utility, consider Judge Stephen Reinhardt's en banc opinion in the same case, where he espouses a type of living constitutionalism to create a constitutional right to assisted suicide.[44] By grounding constitutional interpretation in the original understanding of the Constitution, originalism provides a concrete foundation for analysis. Without such a bedrock principle, the answers to many constitutional questions would be open to debate.[45]

Equally important as the positive answers originalism provides are its negative implications. Even in the areas where originalism offers no clear answer, adherence to the original understanding constrains judges by narrowing the range of possible answers.[46] For example, a purely originalist judge would not engage in the kind of freewheeling analysis at work in *Griswold v. Connecticut*, creating constitutional rights with only the slightest semblance of a textual hook.[47] Thus "entire ranges of problems and issues are placed off-limits." By anchoring the judiciary's authority in the original understanding of the Constitution, originalism seeks to confine the realm of judicial supremacy to those areas where the original understanding is ascertainable. The result, in theory, is judicial deference to democratic majorities in areas where the Constitution is silent or uncertain. Judge Bork explains the idea well: "Where the law stops, the legislator may move on to create more; but where the law stops, the judge must stop."[48]

Even the most ardent proponents of originalism admit that it sometimes fails to constrain judges, but their retort, to paraphrase Winston Churchill, is that originalism is the worst constitutional theory except for all the others. The choice in constitutional theory is not between originalism and a perfect theory; it is between originalism and the nonoriginalist theories. Both approaches are flawed. The question is which flaws are more glaring. As Justice Scalia put it, originalism is "the lesser evil." And because it is true that "for the vast majority of questions the answer is clear" from the text and history of the Constitution, an originalist judge is constrained from holding, for example, that the death penalty violates the Eighth Amendment. This is not to say that originalism provides easy answers for all constitutional questions. The original understanding of such a broad and vague phrase as "the executive Power" is certainly open to debate.[49] Originalism constrains judges only weakly in these areas. But, in the words of Judge Bork, originalism is "simply the best we can do."[50]

In much the same way, Justice Scalia argues that the main danger in constitutional interpretation is that "judges will mistake their own predilections for the law." The nonoriginalist theories that proceed from fundamental values or other vague formulations "play[] precisely to this weakness." It is difficult to distinguish between one's personal political values and the values fundamental to the Constitution or to society, and thus the nonoriginalist theories exacerbate this most dangerous weakness of the judiciary. Scalia asserts that originalism, by contrast, "does not aggravate the principal weakness of the system." Rather, the main defect of originalism is that historical research is often inconclusive, but this flaw will, according to Justice Scalia, "lead to a more moderate rather than a more extreme result."[51] Here one may applaud the originalists for not claiming too much. In their view, originalism and the nonoriginalist theories are vulnerable to the weaknesses of the judiciary, but unlike living constitutionalism, originalism explicitly discourages the conceit that the judge's own values embody the enlightened legal order.

Treating the Constitution as a Source of Law

Originalism also provides a potential check against judicial activism by directing judges to consult an external source—namely the Constitution—for principles of law.[52] A judge must consult an external source for his inquiry to be legitimate, because the judge himself is charged with being an interpreter of law, not its creator.[53] The idea that an external source must be consulted is important because, by definition, it would seem to rule out the judge himself as a source of superior wisdom.[54] Perhaps this external source will sometimes direct judges to use their discretion, but it will still be the law, not the judge's own predilections, dictating when discretion is appropriate. By recognizing that ultimate legal authority stems from sources external to the judge, originalism constrains judges and strengthens their resolve to show restraint.

Furthermore, because originalism properly views the Constitution as simply another source of law, constitutional interpretation becomes a familiar form of legal reasoning, not some exotic species of analysis. Originalist constitutional interpretation bears remarkable similarities to interpretation of statutes, precedents, contracts, and other legal sources that judges work with every day.[55] The alleged simplicity of originalism is that judges perform this same analysis "when they apply a statute, a contract, a will, or, indeed, a Supreme Court opinion to a situation the Framers of those documents did not foresee."[56]

John Hart Ely, a prominent critic of originalism, acknowledges this virtue:

> In interpreting a statute, . . . a court obviously will limit itself to a determination of the purposes and prohibitions expressed by or implicit in its language. Were a judge to announce in such a situation that he was not content with those references and intended additionally to enforce, in the name of the statute in question, those fundamental values he believed America had always stood for, we would conclude that he was not doing his job, and might even consider a call to the lunacy commission.[57]

Ely succeeds in capturing the unquestionable assumption of the public, and indeed the judiciary, that traditional legal analysis is the proper course in statutory cases. But it must not stop there. Originalism acknowledges the Constitution is a higher species of law, but it remains law nonetheless, with all the constraining force we expect from it. If judges instinctively view the Constitution thusly, they will bring to the task of interpretation a familiar toolkit.

For judges have honed their analytical skills on legal texts their entire careers. When confronted with a constitutional issue, originalist judges do not have to transform themselves from traditional legal analysts to fundamental-value diviners. Instead, they apply a familiar form of legal analysis to the case at hand. And although originalist analysis is admittedly not identical to statutory analysis, the overlap is enough to yield dividends.[58] The skills judges learn from sifting through legislative history, it is claimed, serve them well when digging through records of the ratifying conventions. Determining the level of generality of a text involves a certain process, regardless of whether that text is a statute or the Constitution. Originalism, perhaps more than any other theory, harnesses the power of the judiciary's expertise and brings it to bear on constitutional questions.

Legitimizing Judicial Review

Originalism has likewise enjoyed some success in legitimizing judicial review. The question of whether the judiciary's role in resolving the Madisonian dilemma was a legitimate one first inspired Bork to develop his constitutional theory. Through originalism, Bork offered a solution to this problem: "The Madisonian dilemma is resolved in the way that the founders resolved it, and the judge accepts the fact that he is bound by that resolution as law."[59] By accepting the Framers' resolution of the Madisonian dilemma, originalism, in theory, allows judges to fulfill their proper role without illegitimately decreeing their own policy preferences into law.[60]

How did the Framers resolve the Madisonian dilemma? There is evidence that the original understanding of the Constitution called for originalist constitutional interpretation.[61] There is also evidence that the Framers themselves envisioned a limited judicial role. For example, the Framers considered a proposal at the Constitutional Convention of 1787 that would have placed veto power over laws in a Council of Revision consisting of the executive and a number of federal judges, but they ultimately discarded the idea. Bork cites the rejection of this proposal as evidence that the judiciary was meant to have no policymaking role, and he relies on Hamilton's assurances that the judiciary would be the least dangerous branch for the proposition that the judiciary was not understood to have the power to fashion novel rights.[62] Although Bork's argument may have a circular ring to it, it does, if the premises are correct, impart the democratic legitimacy of the Constitution to the courts.[63] If the courts are merely enforcing the Constitution as the Framers intended, then the legitimacy problems should be directed at the Constitution itself, not the judicial messengers.

Achieving Broad Acceptance of Historical Inquiry

Originalism, or at least a watered down version of it, enjoys what perhaps no other constitutional theory can claim: widespread acceptance. As Professor Sanford Levinson observed, "[A]t some suitably abstract level almost everyone is an originalist in at least some limited sense."[64] There is a consensus among constitutional theorists of all stripes that the original understanding of the Constitution is relevant to constitutional analysis.[65] Even the most ardent opponents of originalism concede the utility of knowing the original understanding. Goodwin Liu, Pamela Karlan, and Christopher Schroeder agree that "a commitment to the underlying principles that the Framers' words were publicly understood to convey" is the foundation of sound constitutional adjudication.[66] Justice Breyer directs judges to "read the [constitutional] text's language along with related language in other parts of the document[,]...take account of its history, including history that shows what the language likely meant to those who wrote it[,]…and look to tradition indicating how the relevant language was, and is, used in the law."[67] Even Justice Brennan made the occasional foray into originalist analysis.[68] None of these critics embrace full-throated Borkean originalism. But it is a tribute to Bork's theory that even its staunchest adversaries recognize a legitimate role for original understanding in constitutional analysis.

THE VICES OF ORIGINALISM

A sad fact nonetheless lies at originalism's heart. For all its virtues, originalism has failed to deliver on its promise of restraint. Activism still characterizes many a judicial decision, and originalist judges have been among the worst offenders. They may sincerely strive to discover and apply the Constitution's original understanding, but somehow personal preferences and original understandings seemingly manage to converge. The fault lies with the theory itself. Originalism, like any constitutional theory, is incapable of constraining judges on its own. And instead of recognizing this flaw, originalism provides cover for significant judicial misadventures. The result is too often a new breed of judicial activism masquerading as humble obedience to the Constitution.

Drawing Certitude from Ambiguity

The chief failure of originalism is that the search for original understanding often fails to constrain judicial choices. The historical evidence is often unclear. With respect to a vast number of controversial constitutional questions, originalism offers only ambiguous historical evidence, if any at all. The result is a theory with such loose analytical boundaries that it can be used to support a variety of outcomes on thorny constitutional disputes.

There is often a wealth of historical evidence concerning the original understanding of a particular part of the Constitution. But this abundance is not an embarrassment of riches. Rather, it sows the seed of interventionism. Though originalism was designed to curtail judicial activism by limiting the available options, in practice it may do exactly the opposite. The problem is that originalist analysis frequently produces evidence on both sides of a constitutional issue.[69] For example, in *Alden v. Maine*,[70] Justice Kennedy and Justice Souter each amassed impressive quantities of historical evidence on the original understanding of the Eleventh Amendment, but they came to opposite conclusions on its meaning.[71] The originalist inquiry certainly did not suffer from a lack of evidence, as demonstrated by page upon page of historical analysis. Indeed, the problem was precisely the opposite. There was so much historical evidence—supporting both sides of the issue—that the justices could not come to a consensus. When the evidence is varied enough to support any position, originalism provides no serious constraints. A judge is free to choose, perhaps at a subconscious level, whatever outcome seems desirable and then support this choice with historical evidence. As Professor Mitchell Berman has noted, "In hard cases, these sources of wisdom conflict, and sometimes judges may have no choice but to allow their own convictions and moral intuitions to guide the selection of which course to follow."[72] Judge Posner drives the point home: "Originalism—at least Bork's originalism—is not an analytic, but a rhetoric that can be used to support any result the judge wants to reach."[73]

Take *U.S. Term Limits, Inc. v. Thornton*, for example, where the Court held that states cannot impose term limits on their members of Congress. The Arkansas constitution prohibited anyone who had already served three terms in the House of Representatives or two terms in the Senate from appearing on the general election ballot as a candidate for the office previously held.[74] But the U.S. Constitution already sets forth specific, and possibly exclusive, eligibility requirements for those two bodies.[75] Both Justice Stevens and Justice Thomas wrote originalist opinions, replete with historical evidence of the original understanding of the Constitution.[76] And yet they arrived at opposite conclusions, because it is unclear what the original understanding was concerning whether states could impose additional eligibility requirements beyond those in the Constitution on their members of Congress.[77] Originalism thus offers no guidance on the issue, setting judges adrift. And in these uncharted waters, the originalist judge may be tempted to latch on to familiar personal preferences for direction.

Compounding this problem of conflicting evidence is that there is no principled way to deem certain sources valid and others not. The historical evidence from the founding era comes from a variety of sources. When these sources conflict, as they often do, it is exceedingly difficult to choose one over the other on objective grounds.[78] Should we consult the records of the Constitutional Convention or the ratification debates?[79] And to what extent may an originalist judge rely on events and writings after the framing, such as Justice Story's *Commentaries on the Constitution*[80] or evidence even into the late nineteenth century?[81] Of course, judges do make these many choices; originalism demands it. But even sincere judges can base these choices on the subliminal cues of personal preference, instead of the neutral principles that originalism supposedly holds dear.

When there is not too much evidence, there is too little. Justice Brennan found this to be the greater vice: "All too often, sources of potential enlightenment such as records of the ratification debates provide sparse or ambiguous evidence of the original intention."[82] Judge Bork admits that "in a few cases, [we know] very little or nothing" about the original understanding of the Constitution. The Ninth Amendment is one example. As Bork explains, "There is almost no history that would indicate what the ninth amendment was intended to accomplish."[83] But this has not stopped judges and scholars from fighting over the few scraps of evidence history has provided.[84] Perhaps these jurists would have been better served by reminding themselves that the search for the original understanding may sometimes be futile if the Framers intentionally "hid their differences in cloaks of generality."[85] But as we have seen, judges often view ambiguous evidence as a mandate to create a plausible original understanding of their own.

No one is immune to the perils of the muddled historical record. Even the estimable Justice Clarence Thomas has fallen prey to originalist activism. In his concurrence in *McDonald v. City of Chicago*, which raised the question of whether the individual states were bound by the Second Amendment, Justice Thomas advocated opening up the Pandora's box of the privileges or immunities clause of the Fourteenth Amendment, resurrecting it as a route to incorporation of the Second Amendment and who knows what other rights. And he fastened the Second Amendment upon the States on originalist grounds: "In my view, the record makes plain that the Framers of the Privileges or Immunities Clause and the ratifying-era public understood—just as the Framers of the Second Amendment did— that the right to keep and bear arms was essential to the preservation of liberty."[86] What is so disquieting is that the historical record is ambiguous on whether the privileges or immunities clause was originally understood narrowly, as granting a small list of relatively benign rights,[87] or broadly, as creating an expansive set of additional fundamental rights.[88] As the opinions in *McDonald* chronicle, there is roughly equal evidence on both sides of the issue.[89] In this situation, Judge Bork is correct: because the privileges or immunities clause "has been a mystery since its adoption," the proper course is to abjure judicial supremacy and exercise restraint.[90] And this is precisely what makes Justice Thomas's *McDonald* concurrence all the more troubling. If originalism can turn its most avid followers into activists, then no one is immune.

Forcing Judges to Do a Historian's Job

Even where there is a digestible quantity of coherent historical evidence, it is often difficult for judges to reconstruct the past. Justice Brennan was right to note that the passage of time distorts how modern judges view records from the founding era: "[O]ur distance of two centuries cannot but work as a prism refracting all we perceive."[91] Skilled historians spend lifetimes grappling with this difficulty. And they bring to their work a sense of context acquired over many years of study. Judges are neither trained nor equipped to conduct this type of inquiry.[92] The result, again, is discretion that is anything but constraining.

The originalist judge must thus first play amateur historian to gain access to the often inconclusive historical evidence.[93] And the inquiry is more than simply one of historical fact, but rather of how the original public understanding of a document written over two centuries ago interacts with modern legal questions in a very precise way. Matching up distant eras is a treacherous business, because those who live in different centuries inhabit very different worlds.[94]

Originalist judges might still have a fighting chance at understanding the history if they operated in a system set up for historical inquiry, but this is not the case. Justice Scalia, a self-professed originalist, admits the incompatibility of historical analysis and the judicial system: "[T]his system does not present the ideal environment for entirely accurate historical inquiry[.] Nor, speaking for myself at least, does it employ the ideal personnel." Again, historians spend years studying a period of time and investigating its nuances. Judges have only months to decide each case, and even that time has to be divided among all the cases on the docket.[95] History professors employ research assistants trained in the tools of historical research. Judges have only their law clerks, and although these newly minted lawyers are intelligent and capable, they are typically unversed in the historian's methods.

The pitfalls of amateur originalist forays into history would by all objective measurements seem daunting, but that has not prevented justices from giving it the old college try. Even liberal justices have tried their hands at this supposedly conservative game, for the open secret of originalism is that everyone can play. Thus Justice Black in 1947 invoked originalist history for the proposition that the Bill of Rights applied in toto through the Fourteenth Amendment to state governments.[96] Justice Brennan himself donned the historian's mantle to promote expansive access to federal court on the part of state inmates seeking the Great Writ of habeas corpus.[97] That these displays of judicial erudition were from a historical standpoint highly suspect[98] did not prevent conservatives from later parlaying originalist inquiries into near-Biblical manifestations of objective truth.[99] But true history is often tentative and qualified, and the danger exists that judicial certitude will do a disservice to both the judicial and historical crafts.

With same-sex marriage and implementation of the health care reform bill on the horizon, the dangers of theoretical misadventures have, if anything, grown more severe. Conservatives, for example, may understandably regard the 2010 health care reform bill as a leviathan crammed with unknown mischiefs, but to invalidate it on originalist grounds will require analysis that had best be better than good. The idea that Congress is constitutionally disabled under the commerce power from regulating activity affecting one-sixth of the national economy strikes me as a heavy judicial lift. Any decision that is less than bulletproof will be seen as a purely political under-taking, a revival of *Lochner*'s freedom of contract theory in origi-nalist guise.

Better to let the democratic process formulate a superior alterna-tive to this most complex of national problems, something the Supreme Court is particularly ill equipped to do. Originalism asks much of the judiciary, and judges who accept the role of amateur historian may soon find themselves overwhelmed by their task. When surrounded by sometimes impenetrable history, it is only human to latch on to something familiar, perhaps something that fits with a preconceived notion of how the law should be. As Professor William Nelson noted, "[A] judge who decides constitutional cases on the basis of credibility [of the historical evidence] is likely to mislead both himself and his audience as to the ultimate basis of his decisions."[100]

Devising Multiple Layers of Discretion

For a judge who successfully runs this gauntlet and emerges with the correct original understanding of the constitutional text—assuming one exists—more temptations lie ahead. The original public understanding of a text is meaningless without also knowing at what level of generality that understanding took place. For example, debates rage about the original understanding of the level of generality of the equal protection clause. Does it forbid discrimi-nation on the basis of race?[101] Or does it only forbid discrimination against African Americans?[102] It is true that Bork proposes a solution to this problem—to assign whatever level of generality the history supports—but this answer simply doubles down on the infirmities of originalist inquiries. The conscientious originalist must now confront all the temptations toward personal preference inherent to originalist analysis not once but twice. First, the judge must find the original public understanding of the general principle—what Bork refers to as the derivation. Then, the judge must conduct a new analysis to define that principle at the proper level of generality.[103] This two-step process, each step of which can be uncertain, doubles the activist enticements of originalist analysis.

Beyond the derivation and definition of a constitutional principle, originalism offers additional activist pitfalls in the application. Application is always a tricky step in legal reasoning, and the more than two centuries that separate the founding era from today further complicate the analysis. A prime example is the 2011 decision overturning California's ban on the sale of violent video games to minors.[104] The justices could not agree on the nature of the originalist inquiry, much less the answer. Many seemed to think James Madison's thoughts were important, but thoughts about what? At oral argument, Justice Alito quipped that Justice Scalia was interested in whether James Madison enjoyed video games. Scalia rejoined that he was interested in Madison's thoughts on violence in general. And in his dissenting opinion, Justice Thomas asserted that the decisive question was what the Founders believed about children. The idea that the entire subject was somewhat removed from Madison's contemplation did not prevent the speculation.[105]

Professor Alexander Bickel observed that, "[A]s time passes, fewer and fewer relevantly decisive choices are to be divined out of the tradition of our founding. Our problems have grown radically different from those known to the Framers...."[106] The result is even more uncertainty, which creates even more space for judicial discretion. And in these spaces personal policy preferences sneak into law, with originalism covering their trail. Even Judge Bork essentially throws up his hands at this problem, resorting at last to a plea for judges to practice intellectual integrity.[107] It is one thing to implore judges to be honest and restrained, but it is quite another to excite the judiciary with the charms of a cosmic theory and then offer a perfunctory warning against the dangers so exacerbated by the theory itself.

Weakening Constraints through Hot-and-Cold Originalism

Another failing of originalism, as Justice Scalia acknowledges, arises because originalism must interact with other aspects of the judicial system: "In its undiluted form, at least, [originalism] is medicine that seems too strong to swallow." The "faint-hearted originalist" thus tempers the theory with a respect for precedent and a refusal to reach outcomes too far afield of the public's sensibilities.[108] But such adulterations weaken originalism's internal coherence and hence its constraining force.

Opportunities for personal preference abound when judges must balance the correct result under originalism against existing precedent. Recall Judge Bork's criteria for when it is appropriate to let incorrect precedent stand: when the prior decision has "become so embedded in the life of the nation, so accepted by the society, so fundamental to the private and public expectations of individuals and institutions, that the result should not be changed now." Bork himself admits that this process is not "mechanical."[109] Deciding when a wrongly decided precedent must continue to stand despite its patent failings leaves much room for discretion and judgment. Judges' personal political preferences cannot help but influence how they strike this balance, all the more so when they are distracted by the promises of a cosmic theory.

Whereas Judge Bork at least confronts the problem of precedent directly, he fails to address originalism's more troubling dilemma, that judges refuse to apply it when it produces what to them are unacceptable results. Stuart Taylor is correct that "even when the original meaning is clear, almost everyone rejects it as intolerable some of the time."[110] Justice Scalia acknowledges that there are

Check Out Receipt

Long Hill Library (LHT)
908-647-2088
www.longhilllibrary.org
Saturday, June 30, 2012 10:21:23 AM

Item: 0100205403791
Title: Constitution 3.0 : freedom and t
echnological change
Material: Book
Due: 7/28/2012

Item: 0100402689788
Title: Cosmic constitutional theory : w
hy Americans are losing their inalienable
right to self-governance
Material: Book
Due: 7/14/2012   7/18/12

Total Items: 2

Long Hill Public Library
917 Valley Road
Gillette, NJ 07933
(908) 647-2088
www.longhilllibrary.org

Renew online at catalog.mainlib.org
or call us to renew by phone!

circumstances where he would not follow originalism: "Even if it could be demonstrated unequivocally that [public flogging and hand branding] were not cruel and unusual measures in 1791 ... I doubt whether any federal judge—even among the many who consider themselves originalists—would sustain them against an eighth amendment challenge."[111]

There are many, many nonoriginalist precedents that have achieved what is probably untouchable status, despite being intensely controversial when they were handed down. This pantheon includes cases like *Mapp v. Ohio*,[112] which required that state trials exclude evidence uncovered in unconstitutional searches; *Reynolds v. Sims* (the "one person, one vote" decision),[113] which mandated that state legislative districts be substantially equal in population; and *Frontiero v. Richardson*,[114] which subjected gender discrimination to heightened judicial scrutiny. The dissents and concurrences in each case give a sense of the novelty of the new rights created by these rulings.[115] But these cases have stood the test of time, and they are now unassailable—and rightly so. Even originalist judges would at most temper these nonoriginalist activist precedents; to do otherwise would be folly.[116] And there's the rub. Pragmatism has, not surprisingly, entered the originalist tent. The originalist judge modulates the strict dictates of the original understanding with pragmatic, consequentialist considerations, including whether or not to accept long-standing, but nonoriginalist, precedent. As we shall see, it is a short step from ad hoc acceptance or rejection of activist precedent to promulgating activist precedent of one's own. Originalism has been infused with pragmatism and discretion through the problems in deriving, defining, and applying legal rules, as well as through the treatment of precedent, and judges armed with such discretion are tempted to turn it to ends of their own.

In addition to deferring to established precedent, hot-and-cold originalism introduces other pragmatic considerations into the analysis. Justice Scalia's jurisprudence in the criminal justice area is one example. In *Crawford v. Washington* he performed an admirable originalist analysis, building a convincing case that the original understanding of the Sixth Amendment prohibited the prosecution from using certain out-of-court witness statements against a defendant unless the defendant had a prior opportunity to cross-examine the witness and the witness was unavailable to testify at trial.[117] But in *Blakely v. Washington* Scalia engaged in only a tepid historical review before holding that judges could not enhance sentences above the state sentencing guidelines maximum based on facts that were not proved to a jury beyond a reasonable doubt.[118] Scalia declined to address the history that cut the other way—namely the traditional (and indeed original) power of legislatures to differentiate what must be determined by a jury from facts that may be found during sentencing by a judge.[119] Justice O'Connor has attacked this line of unoriginalist analysis, noting that the "Court has long recognized...that the legislature's definition of the elements of the offense is usually dispositive"[120] and criticizing the *Blakely* majority for citing only "a handful of state decisions in the mid-19th century and a criminal procedure treatise [that] have little if any persuasive value as evidence of what the Framers of the Federal Constitution intended in the late 18th century."[121] Scalia's hot-and-cold originalism grants the justice the discretion to decide when pragmatic considerations, whatever they may be, allow a departure from originalist orthodoxy. And, as we have seen, this discretion dilutes originalism's constraining power.

Perhaps originalism in a pure state, untainted by the hands of mortals, would provide some of the constraints our system needs. But cosmic constitutional theory is for humans, not the gods. The designer of a product that proves to be too complicated and demanding for its purchasers does not blame the customers. He goes back to the drawing board. But the grand theorists of originalism have not taken that tack. Instead, originalists settle for patchwork fixes that may alleviate short-term discomfort but cause long-term instability. Faint-hearted or hot-and-cold originalism "gives away most of the qualities that purported to make originalism appealing in the first place."[122] These innumerable exceptions to originalism's commands are "an invitation to unbridled subjectivity" and, consequently, more judicial activism.[123]

Recently originalism has provided cover for episodic activism. In so doing, the originalists, perhaps unwittingly, helped to validate Justice Brennan's assertion that originalism is "arrogance cloaked as humility" or, in other words, activism cloaked as restraint.[124] Originalism suffers from the same problems as the theories it condemns, namely, that it allows judges enormous discretion that has in fact been wielded for activist ends. And the unfortunate part about it all is that originalism, perhaps more than other cosmic theories, provides cover for discretionary interventions into the democratic process that might otherwise not take place. Our theories are convincing us that we are being objective when broad daylight reveals that we are not.

There is nothing intrinsically wrong with gaps between theory and practice. Indeed, they are unavoidable. The question is whether the gap between theory and practice leads to salutary outcomes or detrimental ones, and with originalism the results are anything but salutary. In the name of a constraining theory, originalism has cast aside restraint. Judges lifted high by the lofty promises of originalism are laid bare to the insidious temptations of personal preference. What is immensely sad is that a theory that was boldly advertised at its inception as a constraining force on the judiciary has been hijacked for unrestrained incursions.

Originalist activism has been prominently on display, most recently with the five-to-four rulings of *District of Columbia v. Heller* and *McDonald v. City of Chicago*. *Heller* announced a strong individual right to bear arms,[125] and *McDonald* incorporated this newfound right against the states.[126] The historical evidence of the original understanding of the Second Amendment is inconclusive. There is support for the proposition that it creates an individual right to bear arms.[127] But there is also plenty of evidence to the contrary.[128] Originalist analysis yields no clear answer. If it did, there would have been no need for the majority to ignore the Amendment's preamble or consult sources from across the ocean or a century after the framing event.[129] What was transparently contestable *Heller* portrayed as indisputable. It drank the elixir of originalism and dismissed the tired old judicial values of humility and restraint.

Disenfranchising democratic majorities across the nation by the narrowest of judicial margins was troubling enough. To do so on the basis of the ambiguous language and inconclusive history of the Second Amendment compounded the difficulties. To surrender the high ground of judicial noninvolvement in intense political controversy disserved the country and the Court. And in bypassing a landmark opportunity to show restraint in the face of apparent preferences to the contrary, originalists missed a chance for statesmanship that may not come again.

In *Heller* and *McDonald*, the majority impaired not only the claim that originalism is a theory of restraint but that it is a theory of limited governance as well. The Rehnquist Court's intervention in the area of firearms regulation at least empowered electoral majorities in the several states,[130] but *McDonald* promptly proceeded to disenfranchise them. The Court henceforth would say what the people of Texas and Rhode Island or Chicago and Tallahassee could and could not enact. The Court as the new ultimate federal authority on firearms would henceforth drown state and local voices out.

One would not have thought it would come to this. But theory preys on a natural weakness of judges—the tendency to substitute their own preferences for those of the Constitution.[131] The unconscious mind is a powerful force, and humans are unparalleled in the art of self-deception. The close historical questions that often arise in originalist analysis are vulnerable to subconscious thumbs on the scale. Originalism's lethal combination of equivocal evidence and emboldening confidence is all the more dispiriting because the hope that it was something different had originally burned so bright.

· · ·

CHAPTER THREE

Political Process Theory: A Third Way Down the Rabbit Hole

So WHAT IS LEFT? For all their popularity, it is clear that neither living constitutionalism nor originalism provides adequate assurances of judicial restraint. Indeed, while proponents of both theories engage in back-and-forth debates over dead hands and democratic accountability, the fact remains that both theories permit (and often encourage) unelected judges to enter the political thickets.

This leaves restraint out in the cold. Yet the need for such restraint lies deep in human and judicial nature. Most of us are wired in the belief that, of course, we are right. Judges in particular become vested in their own views with time. No electorate forces us to make adjustments. We are the kings and queens of our realms. All rise as we walk into the courtroom; no one is to interrupt the Honorable Judges as we hold forth in our robes from an elevated perch.

This accumulation of tokens of our majesty makes it more difficult to practice restraint and more imperative to have internal checks in place. Especially in constitutional cases, the first question should be not "What do I decide?" but "May I in fact decide?" And in all cases, we must ask: might not the views of others be equal or superior to our own? These are questions that do not arise naturally or produce honest answers frequently. Most of us pose these questions only fitfully and episodically. All of us know we should do so all the time. But the struggle for restraint remains essentially a struggle against nature, and the stakes for self-governance have seldom been so high.

Much of cosmic theory was conceived as an ally in this struggle, a counterweight to the certitudes that grab the Solons of the bench. But as we have seen with originalism, things did not work out as hoped. Other theories were likewise launched with much fanfare, each drawn to the Constitution's intriguing structure and irresistible heights.

Enter John Hart Ely's seminal *Democracy and Distrust*. Starting from the premise that the debate between living constitutionalism and originalism rests on a "false dichotomy," Ely offers the seductive promise of a third way: a theory of constitutional interpretation that is equally a theory of judicial restraint. Under Ely's theory, judges should simply stop scrutinizing the substantive outcomes of the legislative process and instead focus solely on the process itself, invalidating laws that clog the arteries of political change or discriminate against minorities without enough political clout to make their voices heard.[1] At first blush, Ely envisions a modest role for judges; so long as the process functions smoothly, their work is done.

At the same time, however, the Court that inspired Ely's work (and Ely himself) is none other than the Warren Court, which was hardly the foremost exemplar of judicial restraint. And while Ely disclaims some of the Warren Court's more controversial decisions, his overall mission is to justify and expand its project. So Ely ends up promising the sun, the moon, and the stars: he suggests that we can have Warren Court results from judges who exemplify restraint.

Like all cosmic constitutional promises, Ely's comes up short. Rather than eschewing value judgments, Ely's theory *requires* judges to make substantive determinations about the nature of American democracy and the wisdom of law. And once judges begin making these value choices, restraint goes out the window. To echo Paul Brest, in Ely's heroic attempt to set forth a cosmic constitutional theory of judicial restraint, he "has come as close as anyone could to proving that it can't be done."[2]

A PRIMER ON POLITICAL PROCESS THEORY

Unlike living constitutionalism or originalism, political process theory as such has not entered the public's vocabulary. It has, however, enjoyed a genuine durability and prominence within the academy. And even in public, process talk abounds, though without reference to Ely by name. Of the great theoreticians, Ely may be the most personally obscure, but a veritable armada of constitutional adventures are rationalized by resort to the process principles that he articulated better than anyone before or since.

The first half of *Democracy and Distrust* canvasses what should now be familiar ground. Rather than take sides in the debate between living constitutionalism and originalism, Ely concludes that neither approach can provide all the answers.[3] For while originalism is "incapable of keeping faith with the evident spirit" of certain constitutional provisions, living constitutionalism turns the Court into a "council of legislative revision," freely substituting its own values for those of the legislature.[4]

To solve the resulting quandary, Ely returns to his unlikely source: the Warren Court. As Ely recognizes, that Court was "'activist' or interventionist" by any measure of the term.[5] But in his view, the Warren Court—the nemesis of most textualists and originalists—did not actually embrace living constitutionalism.[6] Instead, the Warren Court utilized a method of constitutional interpretation predicated on footnote four of Justice Stone's opinion in *United States v. Carolene Products Co.*, an otherwise quotidian case upholding a federal statute prohibiting the interstate shipment of filled milk. In that footnote, the Court suggested that judges should apply close scrutiny when legislation "appears on its face to be within a specific prohibition of the Constitution," "restricts those political processes which can ordinarily be expected to bring about repeal of undesirable legislation," or exemplifies "prejudice against discrete and insular minorities."[7] In short, courts should focus their attention on process rather than outcomes, ensuring both that our democratic government functions openly and transparently and that majorities adequately consider the interests of minorities.

Ely spends a good deal of the remainder of *Democracy and Distrust* making the case for this "participation-oriented, representation-reinforcing"[8] school of judicial review. Lawyers, in his estimation, "genuinely...have a feel" for questions of process, and restricting them to such questions ensures that value judgments are made by democratically elected officials.[9] But more than that, Ely suggests that his method of constitutional interpretation accords with the nature of the Constitution itself. After parsing its text, Ely states that the Constitution is "principally, indeed...overwhelmingly, dedicated to concerns of process and structure and not to the identification and preservation of specific substantive values."[10] When the Constitution has enshrined substantive values, they have either been "so obscure that they don't become issues"[11] or, like Prohibition, so disputatious as to lead to prompt repeal.[12]

Having made the case for his theory, Ely concludes *Democracy and Distrust* by setting forth the parameters of process-based review.

To begin with, Ely argues that courts should intervene only when the "political market... is systematically malfunctioning."[13] In other words, courts should look out for laws that create the risk of legislative entrenchment, such as speech restrictions designed to handicap political challengers.[14] Of course, such an approach to judicial review does not ensure that the legislature will always pass agreeable laws, but that is beside the point. As Ely puts it, "I'm not saying we may not still end up with a fair number of clowns as representatives, but at least then it will be because clowns are what we deserve."[15]

Ely does not stop there, though. He recognizes that a fair process is no guarantee of equality. While any system of democratic governance will produce winners and losers, ceding the fate of the country to simple majoritarianism might end up permanently barring minorities from meaningfully participating in democracy or from sharing its benefits.[16] Hence the need for a mode of judicial review designed to smoke out improper prejudice against "discrete and insular minorities."[17] Under this approach, courts should intervene when legislators "inflict inequality for its own sake" and target groups that are "the object of widespread vilification." But they should also step in when legislators rely on self-serving generalizations about underrepresented minorities.[18] Such "we-they" situations—or as Ely refers to them, "us" vs. "them" situations—raise the grave risk that legislators will overestimate the validity of an ugly stereotype while underestimating its costs.[19] Of course, Ely points out that merely identifying impermissible stereotypes is only part of the inquiry; courts must then apply searching scrutiny to determine whether the classification is unconstitutional.[20] To illustrate that point, he takes on controversial topics like alienage, affirmative action, gender discrimination, and sexual orientation discrimination, reaching scattershot results.[21]

As Ely points out in closing, a focus on process means that courts will sometimes have to tolerate what seems intolerable.[22] But in his view, truly unpalatable laws are unlikely to make it through a fair and open process in the first place.[23] One need not inquire, for example, whether the abolition of marriage is unconstitutional, because such a bill would never be enacted. Once judges ensure the health of our democratic process, their task is largely complete.[24] Hence the allure of Ely's theory, at least on its face: unlike his cosmic predecessors, Ely leaves nobody unhappy. To use a tired metaphor, judicial conservatives get the promise of judges who just monitor the strike zone, while judicial liberals get a strike zone wide enough to accommodate some favorite results. Process theory, it seems, is panacea.

THE VIRTUES OF PROCESS THEORY

For reasons that will soon become clear, Ely's theory has few modern disciples, at least in its most full-throated version. But it is well to take a moment to appreciate the benefits of his work. Whatever its role in contemporary judicial decisionmaking, political process theory has been one of the most frequently discussed and influential theories in the legal academy.[25] Moreover, while process theory ultimately fails to meet its cosmic promises, it has plenty of helpful insights to offer.

Respecting Process as a Constitutional Value

At bottom, the fundamental insight of *Democracy and Distrust* is that process matters. The legitimacy of any government depends on the openness and fairness of its methods. Every election or piece of legislation will produce "winners" and "losers"—those happy with the outcome and those dissatisfied. Yet when the democratic process functions smoothly, the losers today can hope to be winners tomorrow. Moreover, all can have confidence that even if their values were not vindicated, their voices were heard. The opposite is no less true; when the process itself "is undeserving of trust,"[26] the public's confidence in our government can only wane.

Perhaps the great contribution of Ely's work, then, is to get judges and lawyers to think more about process. As the historical exegeses in the *Roe* and *Heller* majorities make clear, the great issues of our day are by no means novel; they are as fractious today as they were at the founding[27] or in ancient Rome.[28] At the end of the day, judges cannot settle these debates. But, as Ely points out, what judges are (perhaps uniquely) capable of doing is assessing the validity of the "processes by which facts are found and contending parties are allowed to present their claims."[29] After all, while we as a nation may never agree on the answers to deeply divisive questions, we can certainly agree that answers that derive from a corrupt process are not worth having.

To be sure, every constitutional theory has to consider process at some point; the text of the Fifth[30] and Fourteenth Amendments[31] forces the issue. But thinking about process in only those contexts risks turning a blind eye to potentially devastating breakdowns. When legislatures enact measures designed to enhance the home-field advantage of incumbency or harm those minorities most susceptible to majoritarian opprobrium, they undermine basic principles of representative democracy and threaten the rule of law. This is not to trivialize individual claims of denials of due process; the Constitution affirmatively requires governments to treat citizens evenhandedly and to some degree to hear them out. But process on a macro level matters too. If the people cannot trust their elected representatives to play by the rules, how can the people have any confidence in the results? It is Ely's contribution to sensitize us to the risks of breakdown in rules—to recognize that there can be no democracy where there is distrust.

Applauding Democratic Virtues

To label *Democracy and Distrust* as merely a book about judicial review is to sell Ely short. While the book's subtitle—"A Theory of Judicial Review"—suggests that its sole concern is the judiciary, *Democracy and Distrust* is about so much more. Underlying Ely's prose is a fierce faith in democratic governance—a belief that the form of government the Founders settled upon is still around today for a reason. Ely closes the book with a rhetorical flourish: "[C]onstitutional law appropriately exists for those situations where representative government cannot be trusted, not those where we know it can."[32] But I think even this understates the strength of his convictions; Ely believes that representative government can generally be trusted. And he views the Constitution in that light, seeking to devise a theory that enables representative democracy to function in the optimal way.

Ely's faith is a breath of fresh air. In contemporary America, at least, originalism and living constitutionalism have turned democracy into a form of weaponry rather than recognizing it as the fundamental organizing principle of our government. Originalists lob the hand grenade of democratic accountability at living constitutionalists, arguing that nine unelected individuals should not impose substantive values on the citizenry.[33] Living constitutionalists respond by firing back the dead-hand fallacy, contending that it is equally undemocratic to let long-dead individuals make value judgments for us.[34] To Ely's credit, he sees this debate as bringing about mutually assured destruction.[35] And rather than pick sides in the argument, he tries to bring it to a close, devising a system of review that ensures we are governed by far more than dead hands or merely nine. Ultimately, however, process theory fails him.[36] Indeed, it may well be impossible to reconcile judicial review and democracy fully; the best we can do as judges is simply attempt to harmonize the tensions as cases arise. Nevertheless, Ely's devotion to representative democracy is commendable; we are better served when we treat democracy as a cherished value rather than as a debating point. Ely's work clearly demonstrates a commitment to democracy that transcends results that displease him.

Recognizing the Importance of Restraint

Our democratic values are not the only thing lost in the debate between originalists and living constitutionalists. Until recently, originalists could claim the high ground in debates about judicial restraint; *Roe* represented the zenith of judicial activism and was without an originalist parallel. No more: *Heller* and *McDonald v. City of Chicago*[37] showed originalism to be susceptible to the temptation of imposing judicial value judgments based on thin and shaky grounds. The current battle between originalists and living constitutionalists, then, seems to be over whose fundamental values are more worthy, not over whether unelected judges should be in the business of declaring fundamental values at all.

But the answer to that latter question should be obvious. For democracy to be true to its name, government must be not just for, but *by*, the people. The Constitution may take certain value choices off the table, but only sparingly; it was and is dedicated primarily to ensuring that the political branches scrupulously represent the wishes of those in whose name they govern. Judges, like all citizens, are entitled to their beliefs, but when they freely substitute those beliefs for the will of the people, they endanger the central tenets of our democracy. Ely makes this point nicely in an observation about his own politics that rings equally true for his opponents: "[O]ne perfectly well *can* be a genuine political liberal and at the same time believe, out of a respect for the democratic process, that the Court

[68]

should keep its hands off the legislature's value judgments."[38] This point is well taken, but Ely is being too careful here—that judges should be cautious in disturbing legislative value judgments is not merely an academic belief but rather the Constitution's unyielding command.

To his credit, Ely talks the talk of judicial restraint. He rightly recognizes that "freedoms are more secure to the extent that they find foundation in the theory that supports our entire government, rather than gaining protection because the judge deciding the case thinks they're important." And he thus seeks to force judges out of the driver's seat when it comes to so-called substantive choices. But Ely's theory cannot fulfill these promises. Political process theory does eschew declarations about guns and abortions, but, as will soon become clear, it nevertheless involves personal value judgments that are different only in degree, if at all. Nevertheless, Ely recognizes that judicial restraint is an organizing principle of our government— that the Constitution leaves the "selection and accommodation of substantive values...almost entirely to the political process."[39] Knowing that may be only half the battle, but half is better than none.

THE VICES OF PROCESS THEORY

Process theory makes some awfully enticing promises: judicial review that promotes self-governance, judges who really do eschew value judgments, and rulings that do not unduly disturb the decisions of the elected branches. Indeed, Ely's promise of judges who act as "referees"[40] is echoed quite clearly in what modern confirmation hearings tell us are the ideal qualities of a good judge.[41] It is no doubt for this reason that Ely's work garners so much academic attention. To quote Paul Brest, process theory is "to constitutional theory what the perpetual motion machine is to science. Hope springs eternal."[42]

But like the perpetual motion machine, or cold fusion, or any scientific innovation that promises to cure all our ills, Ely's promise is ultimately too good to be true.[43] Process theory may condemn the language of fundamental rights and the theory of substantive due process, but it cannot extricate itself from the thicket of value judgments. For process theory to function, the judiciary must reach decisions about what our democracy does and should look like, about which forms of process are important and which less so, about which groups are "discrete and insular," and about which government interests are sufficient to justify process-damaging laws. These decisions are no less divisive or controversial than the ones Ely condemns. After all, empowering judges to make such "process" judgments does not make judicial review any more democratic; it simply moves the ball between the shells. Ely's theory, however, makes this endeavor ever more hazardous; disguising value judgments as questions of process means giving those making them a veneer of restraint. But modesty is precisely what is missing; in this shell game, process is to all intents and purposes substance, and our democratic values end up as the mark.

Allowing Courts to Define Our Democracy

Ely's theory promises to cabin judicial review to a few discrete situations. With respect to "participation-oriented" judicial review, Ely limits judicial intervention to situations where legislators attempt to entrench themselves in office or delegate excessive authority to administrators.[44] This sounds tame enough. But it leaves one big question unanswered: which processes should the courts in fact police? Take the United States Senate, for example. It has come to function by original design and subsequent custom as a brake upon the House of Representatives. Partly as a result, it contains a number of practices that can fairly be characterized as antimajoritarian. Senate rules require sixty votes, for example, to cut off debate.[45] Presidential nominations have been the subject of lengthy individual holds.[46] And both houses of Congress generally award committee chairmanships on the basis of seniority.[47] All these practices have at one time or another been the targets of reformist zeal, and all would appear to be candidates for Ely's disapproval on the grounds that they "chok[e] off the channels of political change."[48]

Yet for courts to go toppling such venerable practices on process theory grounds entails making substantive judgments about what antimajoritarian features properly belong in a democracy, and indeed, in a larger sense, what democracy itself should look like.[49] This only goes to show that procedural judgments can be every bit as subjective and consequential as substantive ones and that such judgments have the distinct potential to place the courts in a partisan light.

Moreover, for courts to readjust the internal processes of a coordinate branch of government raises serious concerns about separation of powers. Because while the Constitution grants to Congress the power to supervise federal judicial structure,[50] a corresponding grant of power to supervise Congress has not been awarded the courts. Thus, as was warned long ago in the context of reapportionment and gerrymandered districts, the danger of tossing judges into the political thicket remains.[51] Gerrymandering is no one's idea of a saintly exercise, and it may exalt the power of a party's base at the expense of coalition politics. But that only raises the question of when and under what criteria courts should overturn gerrymandered districts, and how they can possibly appear nonpartisan in doing so.[52] Process theory solves none of these problems. Indeed, it aggravates them. One could, I suppose, seek to differentiate between internal legislative processes and external electoral processes, confining courts to the latter, but merely suggesting this distinction raises questions of categorization and the relative importance of the categories to the functioning of democracies.[53] This sort of framework can hardly be considered one of judicial restraint.

This only begins to express the difficulties with political process theory. Ely's examples of process review in action raise as many questions as they answer. For example, Ely argues that excessive legislative delegation to agencies is problematic because it allows legislators to avoid accountability for their actions. This view is far from novel; the Supreme Court has long recognized the dangers of government by unelected administrators. Ely echoes those qualms when he says that "letting the experts decide...is an argument for paternalism and against democracy."[54] But letting experts decide has its advantages in an ever more complex and specialized society, and those advantages do not seem especially undemocratic when Congress can restrict or even retract its delegation. The devil has always been in the details; try as it might, the Court has been unable to divine a coherent principle to sequester good delegations from bad.[55] Ely is no different. For all his lofty rhetoric about nondelegation, he does not answer the most critical question: exactly *when* is delegation too much? With no answer to that query, Ely at best invites judges to serve as a roving commission second-guessing the legislature's policy decisions. At worst, process theory gives judges another tool to strike down delegations to those agencies that courts simply do not like.

Similar issues are raised by Ely's discussion of an anti-entrenchment approach to the First Amendment. In easy cases, his framework is simple enough to apply. If legislators attempted to pass a law preventing their opponents from airing political advertisements, courts applying process theory would know exactly what to do.[56] But as is so often the case with cosmic constitutional theory, easy cases have a tremendous ability to deceive. When confronted with more complicated cases, process theory begins to crumble. The Court's recent decision in *Citizens United v. FEC* is illustrative. In *Citizens United*, the Court invalidated the portions of the Bipartisan Campaign Reform Act of 2002 (BCRA) banning corporations and unions from spending general treasury funds on "electioneering communication[s]."[57] In *McConnell v. FEC*, the Court had upheld such limitations,[58] relying on *Austin v. Michigan State Chamber of Commerce*,[59] an earlier precedent holding that political speech "may be banned based on the speaker's corporate identity."[60] But in *Citizens United*, the Court concluded that *Austin* no longer rested on solid doctrinal ground, emphasizing that "[p]olitical speech is 'indispensable to decisionmaking in a democracy,'" regardless of the source.[61]

At first glance, *Citizens United* appears to be precisely the type of result Ely would applaud. If process theory stands for anything, it would seem to be "the more speech the merrier." The provision of BCRA at issue limited political speech by corporations. Under Ely's theory, any decision by incumbents to impose restrictions on political speech raises red flags.[62] While BCRA handicaps incumbents and challengers alike, the fact that legislators voted to approve it suggests that it aligns with their interests in retaining office. And even to the extent Ely credited the avowed legislative purposes of minimizing corruption and distortion, he likely would have objected to protected speech being "proscribed because of fears of how people will react to it."[63] So Ely's successors at Stanford Law School may be right in imagining his sardonic response to statutes like BCRA: "Talk about foxes guarding henhouses."[64]

On closer inspection, though, the matter is not quite so clear-cut. BCRA sought to redress the imbalances of power and wealth between corporate and individual speakers. By striking down the restrictions on corporate political speech, the Court arguably exposed the political process to "potentially deleterious effects."[65]

For one thing, adding the weapon of corporate speech to incumbent candidates' already formidable arsenal might well consign even strong challengers to a quick and hasty end. Moreover, as advocates of campaign finance reform have argued, encouraging candidates to rely on "more numerous and smaller contributions" could head off the looming risk of plutocracy.[66] Indeed, as Justice Stevens observed in his *Citizens United* dissent, corporations are not "natural persons, much less members of our political community," and allowing them to "dominate our democracy" can cause citizens to "lose faith in their capacity... to influence public policy."[67] To the extent corporate speech has these effects, allowing it unfettered access to our political discourse clogs rather than clears the channels of political change.

So which way does process theory cut?[68] Did the *Citizens United* Court befriend free speech or smother small voices? On a case of great magnitude, the judge's own values would drive the outcome. My point, then, is not to second-guess the result that Ely or the Court would reach. It is simply to stress that political process theory is not a neutral form of adjudication that removes value-laden discretion from judging. A theory that provides justification for completely contradictory results is really just a cover for the justices' own beliefs.

Disguising Substance as Process

The number of value judgments involved in "[p]olicing the [p]rocess of [r]epresentation" is enough to cast a shadow over Ely's promises of judicial restraint. Yet the theory enters even murkier waters in the "representation-reinforc[ement]" arena. As usual, Ely starts from an agreeable premise: legislative acts motivated by out-and-out prejudice are at least constitutionally suspect, if not downright unconstitutional. As he puts it, the goal is to ensure that "a different set of rules" is not "being applied to the comparatively powerless."[69] Ely's expansion of that principle, however, opens the floodgates. Ely rightly recognizes that condemning the use of stereotypes in general would make the legislative task impossible; laws designed to govern as vast a country as ours must always rely on generalizations.[70] Instead, Ely suggests that we should only apply heightened scrutiny to stereotypes of the "we-they" variety, where legislators "seiz[e] upon the positive myths about the groups to which they belong and the negative myths about those to which they don't."[71]

Read aggressively, this idea could undo almost every legislative classification on the books. The we-they principle makes it all too easy for disenchanted plaintiffs to change their verboten substantive rights claims ("You denied me the right to do X") into political process claims ("You drew a distinction between people who do and do not do X").[72] After all, the entire criminal law is based on "we-they" distinctions; most crimes involve acts that legislators have never and will never commit. And that is just the beginning. Our legislatures are disproportionately populated by men and women of means, meaning that any law directly or indirectly benefiting the rich or disadvantaging the poor—be it the repeal of the estate tax or the chronic underfunding of public assistance—must also fall under the lens of we-they scrutiny. Aside from the slippery task of discerning who is "we" and who is "they," Ely's formulation presages a constitutional law of class warfare.

Ely does not leave this latter charge unaddressed. Recognizing that we-they analysis is potentially limitless, Ely tries desperately to whittle it down. In his view, we-they analysis "isn't likely to possess a great deal of relevance" to the poor, "since laws that actually classify on the basis of wealth...are extremely rare." What is more likely to disadvantage the poor, Ely says, are "failures to provide the[m]...with one or another good or service." And laws with such effects "do not generally result from a sadistic desire to keep the miserable in their state of misery, or a stereotypical generalization about their characteristics"—meaning they are not constitutionally suspect.[73]

Ely is on the run here. His demonstration of we-they review in action only deepens the confusion of why some we-they laws survive and others don't. According to Ely, criminal laws "plainly should survive," because there is a "patently...substantial goal" behind them. Laws that discriminate against racial minorities are impermissible, whereas laws that benefit them pass muster, ignoring the possibility that the "they" in affirmative action plans may be other minorities or relatively disadvantaged whites. Gender discrimination is allowed, so long as the laws in question were passed after women began to attain political power, though Ely does not tell us exactly what the operative date is for such claims. And laws that decline to recognize same-sex marriage are presumably constitutionally infirm; while legislators interact with gays and lesbians frequently, negative stereotypes about them will abound so long as prejudice makes them reluctant to disclose their sexual identity.[74]

The question of same-sex marriage in fact poses a formidable challenge to Ely's process theory. As a matter of policy, it seems quite wrong for this country to accept the enormous contributions of gays and lesbians to our civic and communal life and then to deny those same citizens the satisfactions and fulfillments of matrimony. But progress from this hurtful state requires democratic assent to be enduring, as well as a recognition that the millennia of experience with marriages as the union of a man and a woman cannot be swept aside by judges operating under "we-they" paradigms. The debate is too profound, the serious arguments on both sides of it too weighty, for any such judicial foray. Far better for Americans to recognize through their many votes and voices that marriage between two loving souls is right and just than for judges to decree the same under the we-they prong of political process theory.

To the extent Ely reaches his conclusions by applying strict judicial scrutiny to certain laws, process theory is no different from any of its competitors. Whether one makes value judgments at the fundamental rights level or while balancing interests and fit, the end result is essentially the same. Either way, judges are bound by nothing more than their own sense of propriety. Indeed, even Ely's staunchest defenders concede the point. For example, in his valiant attempt to rescue process theory, Michael Klarman admits that Ely's applications "give[] away the ballgame," as "distinguishing justifiable from unjustifiable disadvantaging quite plainly requires a substantive value choice."[75] Ely's critics, on the other hand, are more pointed; in the words of Samuel Issacharoff, "[M]oving first base back five feet does not eliminate close plays, it just changes where they occur."[76]

In sum, Ely's theory does not make judges into impartial umpires. They remain players on the field. Ely's discussion of the death penalty is telling. He acknowledges that as a teenager, he would argue "to or with anyone who would listen the immorality of capital punishment." And while he claims that his "resolution on the issue has softened," he ultimately arrives at the same result that he would have as a young man. In Ely's view, the death penalty presents an "inescapable equal protection problem.... It is so cruel we know its imposition will be unusual."[77] Nobody would deny that the death penalty is contentious, nor should anyone begrudge Ely his views. But whether unconscious or not, the congruence between Ely's personal views and the products of his analysis undercuts the notion that his theory encourages judicial restraint. In that light, one can be forgiven for believing that political process theory, for all its soothing rhetoric, is no more restrained than its cosmic competitors.

Imagining a Constitutional Warrant

The final and perhaps broadest difficulty with process theory is none other than the precise legal basis for it. To invoke footnote four of the Supreme Court's *Carolene Products* decision as a foundation for process theory is the height of insider parlance. While one might visit a class in constitutional law and find students conversant with its meaning, most Americans would rightly shake their heads in wonder. It's asking a bit much of a footnote to answer the question of what explicit statutory or constitutional authority exists for the type of freewheeling political judgments Ely's process review entails.

To be sure, statutes like the Administrative Procedure Act give courts some authority to curb the denial of due process on the part of administrative agencies.[78] And the due process clause of the Fourteenth Amendment obviously draws courts into process when due process is denied to "any person."[79] But these enactments speak of process more in a micro sense and do not invite courts into the broad, macro-process judgments Ely would have them adjudicate. Indeed, the fact that the Framers and Congress alike thought to enact provisions allowing judges to engage in process review in certain discrete situations belies any contention that the Constitution gives judges a general warrant to insert themselves into the political process.

Instead, the Constitution at most gives judges specific authority to redress violations of specific provisions. But even in that context, courts must exercise great caution before injecting themselves into the vortex of varied political questions. Judges convinced of their duty to intervene when the " 'market'...is systematically malfunctioning" and their ability to "objectively...assess claims" of political process failure might well view themselves as ideal arbiters of thorny separation of powers questions.[80] But the idea that courts, for example, should referee on process grounds disputes between the legislature and executive over the respective realms of their authority is one so fraught with difficulty that I expect most students of the Constitution would not advise it. It is often far preferable to allow the political institutions under our Constitution to struggle among themselves, with each bringing to bear the respective arsenal of powers the Framers accorded them.

In the end, Ely's claim that judges are "experts on process"[81] is true to a point. But just because the Constitution references process does not mean that it establishes the judiciary as a board of process review.[82] Indeed, I suspect the apogee of process arbitration is in some respects the case of *Bush v. Gore*.[83] Whatever one's view of whether the Florida recount process went awry, the Court's decision to cut short that recount on contestable equal protection grounds cannot be hailed as a model of judicial restraint. And if process theory encourages courts to weigh in on such matters as who should be our next president, that theory is no friend of self-governance. Moreover, to the extent Ely views restraint as a noble judicial characteristic, he overlooks the fact that courts are adept at using process to *augment* their authority, either by acting as none too dispassionate referees or by requiring so much process as to wear public officials down and reduce them more nearly to a point of paralysis. In short, process theory can be viewed as exactly the opposite of what it is advertised to be. It is a prescription for an emboldened judicial role unsupported by the Constitution and covered by little more than a fig leaf of restraint.

CHAPTER FOUR

Pragmatism: Activism through Antitheory

THE CONSTITUTIONAL THEORIES outlined above can neither secure restraint nor safeguard self-governance. Perhaps as a result, Judge Richard Posner, constitutional theorizing's most vocal critic, has proposed an alternative view of pragmatic adjudication.[1] An intellect for all seasons, Posner has sought to demystify, to replace a priesthood with a practical fraternity, albeit one with legal skills. Judge Posner is right to argue that the existing theories cannot do the difficult work of constraining the judiciary. But his pragmatic alternative gives short shrift to the values of traditional adjudication. It is a formless approach that leaves judges adrift in a sea of legislative discretion.

THE PERPETUAL FAILURE OF CONSTITUTIONAL THEORIES

Judge Posner harbors well-known suspicions about constitutional theorizing. The Constitution, the most important datum in any constitutional theory, does not lend itself to categorization or simplification; it is "full of contradictions and ambiguities, sources of endless contestation." Ambiguity in text and contradiction in precedent, the high stakes involved, and the emotional salience of the issues make constitutional adjudication the "least disciplined" area of American law.[2] As a result, in many constitutional cases judges will inevitably be left with significant discretion.[3] And even with cleaner doctrines, constructing constitutional theory would be a perpetually unfinished project:

> [C]onstitutional theory has no power to command agreement from people not already predisposed to accept the theorist's policy prescriptions. It has no power partly because it is normative, partly because interpretation, the subject of constitutional theory, is not susceptible of theoretical resolution, and partly because normativists in general... do not like to be backed into a corner by committing themselves to a theory that might be falsified by data....[4]

Finally, even if someone surmounted these obstacles and created the One True Theory, Posner argues we would remain in the dark: there are no mutually accepted principles for choosing among theories, leaving us unable to sift the theoretical wheat from the chaff to find the truth.[5] We are fated therefore to an "interminab[le]," irreconcilable constitutional debate.[6]

Posner does not mince words or disguise his disdain for contemporary cosmic constitutional theories. None of them "have any... real intellectual depth,"[7] being instead "rationalizations of decisions based on other grounds," "rhetorical weapons,"[8] or, most disturbingly, "mainly just rationalizations of their authors' political ideolog[ies]."[9] Constitutional theories thus do worse than fail— they provide troublesome cover for judging by ideology instead of neutral principles. Although we may be stuck with theory-building,[10] we should stop thinking that "judges can be bludgeoned into agreeing to adopt one of the constitutional theories" and look for other ways of guiding or living with their inevitable discretion in constitutional cases.[11]

So what should judges do? Posner argues that what they often in fact do is decide pragmatically.[12] Pragmatic judges do not feel themselves bound by any duty to follow constitutional text or precedent.[13] Rather, they focus on the future, "basing... judicial decision[s] on the effects the decision[s] [are] likely to have, rather than on the language of a statute or of a case, or more generally on a preexisting rule."[14] Pragmatism itself does not supply the metric for determining which results are the best results—the individual judge does—but Posner is confident that there is enough homogeneity among judges that their value judgments will often produce acceptable consensus.[15]

Posner's position is best understood through his attempts to distinguish pragmatism from such things as case-by-case balancing, equitable judging, and imposing one's policy preferences. The pragmatic judge takes no overall position on case-by-case balancing. Individual fact finders may consider all relevant information (thereby enhancing decisionmaking), but rules provide clearer notice and easier adjudication. The trade-offs between fact-based and rule-based adjudication depend on the context. It would be unpragmatic to declare a hard preference for one or the other.[16]

Similarly, the truly pragmatic judge rejects deciding cases through homespun equity. Pragmatic judges consider *overall* consequences, not just those falling on the litigants. A plaintiff whose predicament may tug at the heartstrings should not blind the pragmatist to outcomes that would create the greatest public good.[17] In other words, "[s]hort-sighted justice is not pragmatic; it has bad overall consequences."[18]

Nor does the pragmatic judge simply impose his policy preferences. Pragmatic judges face constraints that significantly, though not entirely, direct their decisions. Text and precedent, though not conclusive, nonetheless offer guidance. As mentioned above, pragmatic judges do not feel duty-bound to follow text, precedent, or tradition. But there are costs to departures. At least in the lower federal courts,[19] a significant number of cases will be so clearly resolved by traditional legal reasoning that "pragmatic" departures would create unpragmatic chaos. Similarly, text and precedent represent sources of possible wisdom, and ignoring them increases the likelihood of error.[20]

Pragmatists are also constrained by the systemic consequences of judicial intermeddling. Parties rely upon predictable legal rules, and this reliance counsels caution. Constitutional text and tradition allow courts' decisions to be perceived as legitimate.[21] Ignoring or fudging that text depletes courts' political capital, harming their effectiveness and, perhaps, society itself.[22] Wise pragmatists such as Posner also refrain from transferring the bulk of lawmaking authority to unelected judges: it's just too dangerous given the significant risk of error involved in adjudicating complex policy issues through bench or jury trials and appellate briefs.[23] Because the "moderate" pragmatist puts appropriate weight on systemic considerations, his votes largely track a traditional moderate's.[24]

But pragmatism does not purport to be a successful cosmic constitutional theory. It prides itself upon being anything but. Rather, pragmatism is what Posner thinks we often do, and what we perhaps should do, given that all else fails. It "is not a machine for grinding out certifiably correct answers to legal questions."[25] In Posner's view, legal decisions within a certain zone of reasonableness cannot be

shown to be "right" or "wrong," and thus pragmatic and nonprag-
matic judges may differ without either being wrong or unreason-
able.[26] Nor does pragmatism provide criteria for determining what
the best consequences are. As a result, pragmatism provides "local
rather than universal" solutions, ones justified by community
consensus rather than logical necessity.[27] Pragmatism admittedly
faces practical problems in gathering data and methodological problems in weighing competing interests.[28] And pragmatism cannot
eliminate the essentially personal factors in judging. Judges will
always have emotions, intuitions, cognitive defects, and ideological
backgrounds that influence pragmatic decisionmaking.[29] But with
these caveats, pragmatism still purports to offer a useful way of
resolving live constitutional issues.

THE VIRTUES OF PRAGMATISM

Given the intellectual firepower of its chief proponent, pragmatism
unsurprisingly boasts real advantages. It provides for flexible adjudication, reminds judges of their limitations, and encourages judicial
candor.

Providing Adjudicative Flexibility

Pragmatism seeks to avoid the pitfalls of rigidity. The Constitution was drafted, ratified, and subsequently amended in circumstances radically unlike our own, and it is not easily changed.[30]
Though the basic constitutional framework has proven remarkably resilient over the last two hundred years, a dogged unwill-
ingness to ever consider the practical differences between now
and then could leave us with eighteenth-century solutions to
twenty-first-century problems or, worse yet, with no solutions at

all. Given the magnitude of the problems we call on the Constitution to solve, pragmatism serves as a safety valve. The Constitution "is not a suicide pact,"[31] and pragmatism helps keep it that way.

The Supreme Court's occasional glances toward pragmatism show its potential benefits. Posner rightly praises Justice Breyer's concurrence in *Van Orden v. Perry*.[32] A decision to strictly enforce a ban on public displays of religious texts such as the Ten Commandments would have been disastrous: "It is hard to imagine not only a more divisive, but also a more doctrinaire and even absurd project" than the purge that would inevitably have followed from the liberal dissenters' hard separationist position in *Van Orden*.[33] In numerous areas the Court has crafted doctrines that instruct courts to look at consequences. Posner notes the clear pragmatic benefits that flow from legal doctrines that delay judicial tinkering.[34] These doctrines go by many names, including standing, absention, and the political question doctrine, and all can be invoked pragmatically to avoid deciding cases where interference with other branches or sovereigns looms too large.[35]

The advantages of pragmatism also show themselves in contexts where pragmatic balancing shapes substantive rights. Balancing the privacy interests of students against the needs of school administrators for discipline and order provides a practical Fourth Amendment framework for school searches.[36] Likewise, balancing personal needs for public assistance against government interests in efficient program administration provides a practical framework for determining how much administrative process a welfare recipient is due.[37] Pragmatism thus admonishes judges to create workable solutions that protect individuals while allowing government to go about its business. A touch of pragmatism usefully keeps courts from plunging in too quickly and from doing more harm than good when they do intervene.

Reminding Judges of Their Limitations

Pragmatism's antitheoretical bent also focuses judges on their own limitations. Posner plausibly argues that bringing judges face to face with the complicated but potentially enormous effects of their decisions may sensitize them to their own cognitive limitations and lack of experience.[38] In this way, pragmatic judges might stay their hands where theory-driven ones would intervene. A diehard originalist might do originalist justice even if the heavens were to fall; the pragmatist would be much less foolhardy in imposing his contested views in light of such dramatic consequences.

Pragmatism's strongly realist take on judges and judging, while problematic, may help convince judges of the legislature's relative superiority. As Posner notes, judges likely lack both the relevant data and the democratic responsiveness needed for effective policy-making, not to mention the ability to appropriately process these scientific and political inputs.[39] By burying appellate judges under mountains of data reminding them of the time, energy, and expertise needed to make competent public policy, pragmatic adjudication helps judges avoid the pitfalls of aggressive theorizing. Posner's pragmatism ultimately fails to deliver this benefit because of its empirical aggressiveness and instruction to judges to seek best outcomes.[40] But a modified pragmatism that reminds judges of legislative capabilities would impress upon judges the difficulty of policymaking and the importance of restraint.

Believing Honesty Is the Best Policy

Pragmatists and their allies marshal impressive evidence that American judicial decisions do not arise from a mechanical application of law to facts. There is significant evidence that judges' political ideologies, the composition of the panels on which they sit, and other nonlegal criteria play some role in decisionmaking.[41] There is also significant anecdotal evidence to that effect from within the judiciary. Posner examines the autobiographical writings of judges and argues that many of them admit to being tugged by pragmatic considerations in deciding cases.[42] There is even evidence that explicit pragmatism is on the rise, as evidenced by a marked jump in references to effects and consequences in statutory interpretation opinions.[43]

These findings point to another potential benefit of pragmatic decisionmaking. If judicial outcomes seem inexplicable or based on undisclosed judicial value judgments, Posner's attempt to tout pragmatism as an accurate and attractive account of American judging would helpfully bring the whole process into the open. Spurred by pragmatism's benefits and by Posner's open defense of them, judges who already place emphasis on consequences in their decisions will feel more comfortable acknowledging that emphasis despite its clash with prevailing traditionalist norms. Such candor would create a more fruitful discussion of judges' proper role; judges would no longer be pretending that their pragmatic or ideologically driven decisions stem from some supposedly neutral theoretical model.[44] Of course, pragmatists tell the truth if—but only if—honesty is the best policy, so increased candor is not certain.[45] But Posner's visibility, combined with the substantial evidence of pragmatism's descriptive strength, suggests that at least some pragmatically inclined judges will open up, allowing a more forthright discussion of their roles and views.

THE VICES OF PRAGMATISM

As any good pragmatist would admit, we have to count pragmatism's cons as well as its pros. Pragmatism has not suffered from a lack of critics. The most important criticism of Posner's pragmatism is that it puts great power in judges' hands and tells them precious little about what to do with it. In this way, pragmatism's methodology provides generous incentives, excuses, and cover for judges to turn away from their duty of restraint and toward the role of aggressive junior varsity legislator.

Deciding Whether to Balance Threatens Restraint

Posner strives to distinguish his pragmatism from its unruly, lawless, and widely condemned activist cousin: widespread use of "totality of the circumstances" tests. He argues that truly pragmatic judges do not decide as if writing on blank slates. If the traditional legal materials clearly resolve a case, the true pragmatist does not generally ask whether the rule applied is pragmatically a good one; the systemic costs of allowing judges to casually ignore text, precedent, or history are too high to encourage judges to reconsider each legal rule afresh.[46] However, if the materials do not resolve the case, the pragmatic judge must embark on the essentially legislative task of creating a desirable solution, with all the balancing of costs and benefits such problem solving involves. Thus pragmatism at first appears to provide a kind of natural restraint: judges generally go about their business of interpreting texts and precedents, but where those fail, judges seek, as their common law ancestors did, to make good policy. In each case pragmatic judges must decide whether to reweigh the legislative balance, and, at least in the lower courts, the answer will generally be "no."[47] We don't need to worry, Posner assures us, about the horrors of perennial, squishy balancing and rebalancing.[48]

But this restraint is illusory, and pragmatism cannot prevent judges from undertaking a balancing act, or, in other words, from adding up pluses and minuses on their own to determine whether an outcome is good or bad. Posner relies crucially on two factors to

stop the slide: the constraining power of the traditional legal materials and the judge's ability to determine where balancing isn't pragmatically worth it. Neither factor is up to the task. With respect to
legal materials in constitutional cases, Posner himself acknowledges
that "[t]here is almost no legal outcome that a really skillful legal
analyst cannot cover with a professional varnish," particularly with
the aid of talented and eager law clerks.[49] Precedent's restraint is
further weakened by constitutional law's unruliness (which Posner
notes[50]) and by the Supreme Court's rejection of stare decisis in
constitutional cases.[51] These factors significantly weaken precedent's power to prevent judges from freely engaging in case-by-case
pragmatic balancing.

The judge's role here only makes things worse. Posner acknowledges that judges bring with them some of the factors that determine the size of their own personal discretionary sphere. Intelligence
plays a role: smarter judges will more easily find the ambiguity that
allows them to balance, and those less gifted will often mistakenly
think they have done so.[52] So too preferences: "A judge can...attach
great weight to the rules of the game that distinguish the judicial
from the legislative role...or [can exhibit]...a degree of disdain for
those rules." The latter judge will have no problem twisting statutes
or stretching precedents to find room for pragmatic balancing.[53] And
pragmatic judges may start by asking themselves what result would
be practically preferable and only then ask whether the traditional
materials block that result.[54] The sequencing of inquiries here likely
influences the outcome; feeling pragmatically led in one direction
increases one's willingness to stretch precedent or take an aggressive position—to abandon restraint.[55] Pragmatists' express disavowal
of any "*duty* to secure consistency in principle with what other
[legislative or judicial] officials have done in the past" only heightens
the concern.[56] We can more readily trust traditional judges to play
by the rules even granting ambiguity and tension; they deeply

believe they should. But pragmatists follow the rules only instrumentally, and instrumentalism won't secure restraint.

Deciding How to Balance Threatens Restraint

The problems involved in determining whether to balance are only exacerbated by the pragmatic balancing process itself. As mentioned above, Posner recognizes that this task is extremely complicated but nonetheless argues that it will often generate consensus: "[P]rovided there is a fair degree of value consensus among the judges, as I think there still is in this country, [pragmatism] can help judges seek the best results unhampered by philosophical doubts."[57] His excessive optimism about pragmatic balancing is reflected in his discussion of *Roe*:[58]

> There may be no objective method of valuing the competing interests. But analysis can be made more manageable by pragmatically recasting the question as not which of the competing interests is more valuable but what are the consequences for each interest of deciding the case one way rather than the other. If one outcome involves a much smaller sacrifice of one of the competing interests, then unless the two are of very different value that outcome will probably have the better overall consequences. That was the approach the Supreme Court took in *Roe v. Wade*, in balancing the mother's interest against the state's interest in fetal life, though the approach was executed ineptly.[59]

The serious difficulties in pragmatic adjudication are rather nakedly on display here, and the result is not pretty. First there is the difficulty of even identifying the relevant interests that the pragmatist must balance. Here, Posner (and the *Roe* Court) seem to suggest that there are essentially two, the mother's interest in not carrying the fetus to term and the state's "interest in fetal life." But what of the other interests at stake? Presumably a pragmatist deciding a case like *Roe* must additionally consider: the value of life to the fetuses themselves, both *in utero* and over the course of their lives if they are not aborted; the psychological harms and benefits to both pro-choice and pro-life camps depending on the outcome; the institutional concerns raised by the Court's use of substantive due process to invalidate state laws; the disparate impact of criminalizing abortion on poor and minority women; the medical risks from a larger number of legalized, safer abortions as compared to a smaller number of illegal, unsafe abortions; and so on. Ironically, pragmatism in this way and others becomes "wildly impractical on its own terms."[60]

But the point is not just that considering all the consequences is impossible, especially within the confines of an adversarial judicial system. More importantly, *Roe* illustrates that from among the welter of possible consequences that should be considered by pragmatic judges, certain ones must be given pride of place because lack of time and knowledge prevents us from considering them all. But that ordering of consequences is neither obvious nor easily grounded in reason or consensus; the *Roe* Court's decision to dodge the metaphysical question of a fetus's status put to the side the one interest pro-life advocates thought was most clearly at stake. The combination of pragmatism's instruction to judges to consider the consequences and the incredible variety of interests and consequences at stake thus creates a no-win situation for judicial restraint. Pragmatism either encourages judges to attempt the impossible feat of balancing all relevant interests, imbuing them with the notion that it is their task to craft the best policy for the nation, or it helps them do with interests what judges are sometimes said to do with legislative history: "look[] over a crowd and pick[] out [their] friends."[61]

Even if one could consider all the interests at stake, it is hard to imagine that the process would generate the consensus Posner foresees.[62] Without that consensus, pragmatic adjudication's claim to resolve cases through something other than just the judge's own preferences becomes more questionable. The cottage industry devoted to disagreeing with Posner's weighing of the consequences provides evidence here. J. Mark Ramseyer contends broadly that pragmatic adjudication itself is not pragmatic because creative judges will "muddy the law" and less capable judges trying to follow them will actually worsen it.[63] David Cole argues that Posner's pragmatic balancing undervalues civil liberties and the harms stemming from their infringement in areas such as electronic surveillance, coercive interrogation, and preventive detention.[64] Cass Sunstein argues that Posner undervalues the stigmatic harms suffered by disabled persons when he casually weighs the costs and benefits of requiring employers to provide accommodations for disabled employees.[65] The list could go on (and on), but even in abbreviated form it demonstrates that seeking "best results" too easily devolves into seeking particular results—namely, the judge's preferred results. Pragmatism, by encouraging judges to engage in this inevitably hazy exercise of balancing, leads both "activists" and more traditionally minded judges into briar patches the courts were never intended to enter.

Finally, pragmatism takes too contrarian a stance toward other actors in the political process. That stance, combined with its strong notion of judicial power and its clamor for empirical evidence, provides significant temptations for judges to forget their place in the constitutional order.[66] Pragmatism demands that judges be fed empirical information about "legislative facts" such as "what economists have learned about competition and labor markets and what criminologists have learned about criminal behavior and punishment."[67] But as Jeffrey Rosen points out, judicial inquiries into such legislative facts are "inherently aggressive": when a judge knows "the facts" and it seems like the always messy legislative process has produced an inadequate product, the temptation to intervene will be strong.[68] Empirical evidence creates a veneer of objectivity similar to what Posner argues other cosmic theories create, even though in the complicated, high-stakes issues involved in important constitutional cases, the "facts" are often murky at best and wrong or partisan at worst.[69]

More importantly, the relationship between empirical facts and legislative judgments is not a technocratic one. Of course, empirical data can be helpful to legislators and judges alike. No one wants a bunch of know-nothings making decisions of huge import. But empirical data is only part of a decision-making process, and not always the most important one. We often leave to legislative discretion decisions that are almost impossible to justify by scientific notions of the public good.[70] And with good reason: legislators must be able to consider their constituents' nonempirical values, as well as their unstatistical fears, to properly represent them in our largely majoritarian system. If those values and fears do not produce legislation that raises everyone's utility or produces "best outcomes," so be it. Legislators also properly indulge in the give-and-take necessary to get things done in a political climate with as many different voices and needs as ours. Arming judges with reams of data and telling them to go about doing empirical good encourages aggressive review and substitutes judicial fiat for representative policymaking.

This aggressive stance is reflected in the activist ideology necessarily underpinning a pragmatic approach. John Manning points out that pragmatism, unlike purported attempts to divine legislative intent, requires a "robust [conception of] judicial power";[71] judges are not merely agents of legislators or Framers but are instead independent policymakers. This view again creates a tendency toward judicial intervention; if one believes that "the practice of interpretation and the general terms of the Constitution...authorize judges to enrich positive law with the...practical concerns of civilized society,"[72] the temptation to exercise that authority will be stronger than if one believes that such enrichment is either a last resort or an impermissible infringement. Such a conception might also lead a judge to look upon a legislature's output less charitably, as the work of an incompetent, bumbling competitor for policymaking supremacy. Posner is careful not to advocate rebalancing when the legislature has already balanced,[73] but pragmatists with a more jaundiced view of the legislative process or a more aggressive disposition may, with the help of this strong notion of their authority, be much more willing to intervene than the dispositionally conservative Posner.[74] Dispositional conservatism is too thin a reed to rely on for restraint, especially when pragmatism gives judges a broad vision of their power and the tools with which to use that power to the detriment of legislator and citizen alike.

Pragmatism as the Antithesis of Restraint

In a way it is unfair to portray Judge Posner as insufficiently attentive to the need for judicial restraint. In fact, he is highly sensitive to the charge that his approach to judging is unrestrained. His academic writings are replete with calls for courts, especially the Supreme Court, to recognize their limitations and defer to other institutional actors.[75] These calls are not, in Posner's mind, inconsistent with pragmatism—indeed, they follow from it. "It would be unpragmatic for a court to invalidate a program as unconstitutional or otherwise unlawful before the program had a chance to prove its worth empirically." Pragmatic judges will also favor narrow grounds of decision and incremental change; such an approach maximizes the space for social experimentation and avoids the unforeseen and negative consequences of hasty, broad decisionmaking.[76] And as emphasized above, the appropriately pragmatic judge considers the long-term, systemic consequences of judicial deviation: "If the judge deviates from the 'legislative judgment' in anything but 'the extreme case,' the ensuing 'guerilla warfare' against the legislature would have a 'destabilizing' effect and would 'in general [be] a bad thing'...."[77] Recognizing the limitations of his own knowledge and the mischievous consequences of tinkering, the true pragmatist rarely intervenes.

Lip service to restraint is one thing. The elements of the theory are something else. And the elements of Posner's view systematically undercut restraint. Pragmatic judges are "forward-looking" and future-oriented,[78] have a "taste for empirical inquiry,"[79] and lack any sense of duty to the traditional sources of legal authority.[80] In a very real sense, these attributes mean pragmatists aren't really judges after all; judges look to the past not just because it is a source of practical insight but because the document to be interpreted was enacted in the past, and looking to it is their job. Unlike the common law judges who served as architects of legal policy, judges in constitutional and statutory cases have more than just good policy to worry about: they must consider the intentions and acts of the representative bodies whose activities brought the courts themselves into being and whose democratic imprimatur gives courts their strength. Pragmatism cuts the bonds to representative institutions by making adherence to enacted law a matter of practical convenience rather than democratic obligation.[81] Pragmatism also weakens courts by telling judges that their task is essentially a backstop version of the legislature's: weighing the myriad systemic consequences of particular choices and adopting the best one.

In addition to this vision of the judge's immense policymaking role, pragmatism provides judges with particularly dangerous tools of interventionism and precious little guidance on how to use them.

Pragmatism's relentless focus on evidence and outcomes tells judges little about what to do once they have decided to improve the people's handiwork. Pragmatism, Posner states, "leave[s] open the criteria for the 'best results' for which the pragmatic judge is striving."[82] But as Eric Rakowski notes:

> Posner exhorts judges to weigh all relevant considerations, from society's interest in stable rules to the economic consequences of competing outcomes to the importance of respecting some nebulous ideal of democratic governance, and to choose whatever result seems most reasonable overall. In the absence of more specific advice on how to appraise these factors, however, this imperative is almost vacuous. And Posner provides only cursory guidance.[83]

It's no surprise Posner can't offer more definitive instructions on how to do the math. There are just too many questions, and they are all too difficult, for the approach to result in anything other than judicial guesswork. In a hypothetical Eighth Amendment case about harsh juvenile sentencing, Posner would have judges ask "about the psychological and social meaning" of juvenile lifetime imprisonment, the "likely impact on [the defendant's] family[] and on the larger society," whether the deterrent effect of such sentences will outweigh the harm to the defendant, whether "utility [is] the right criterion here," as well as numerous other intractable questions. Representative bodies and expert commissions deliberating over thousands of pages of evidence could not easily find sensible answers to such questions; it would be miraculous if a federal judge could do so after a five-day bench trial. Posner admits as much, accepting that a judge's "response [to such a case] is bound in the end to be an emotional rather than a closely reasoned one...."[84] Although Posner views this as our inevitable fate, it is the pragmatic process itself that brings it on: by assigning judges a role they were not intended to have and then by asking judges to pose questions they cannot answer.

In the end, then, supposedly antitheoretical pragmatism turns out to be just like the other cosmic constitutional theories. It does sound more modest in its pretensions, admitting that it is "not a machine for grinding out certifiably correct answers to legal questions" and that it will often generate inconclusive results.[85] But all cosmic constitutional theories note the difficulty of application and the existence of reasonable disagreement.[86] None, including pragmatism, channels that realization into a proper recognition of the limited judicial role. Like living constitutionalism, pragmatism ascribes to judges a role that is beyond their democratic authority by transplanting the methodology and vision of common law adjudication into the inhospitable soil of modern constitutional law. Like originalism and political process theory, pragmatism places in the hands of judges a methodology at once deceptively objective and impossible to deploy.

An Illustration of Pragmatism's Failings

There remains the difficulty that pragmatism can fall into the wrong hands. We have noted earlier that Posner is himself a dispositionally conservative judge more or less inclined toward restraint. Yet Posner is not the only pragmatist out there. Cass Sunstein, Posner's former colleague on the University of Chicago Law School faculty, propounds a theory called "minimalism" that Posner himself admits is "close to [his] own preferred stance."[87] Sunstein's illustrations of minimalism in action reveal just how few constraints pragmatism actually places on judges and display how pragmatism can, in certain hands, embody the abdication of restraint.

At its core, Sunstein's theory rests upon a simple premise: judges must strive to issue the narrowest rulings possible. As Sunstein puts it, judges should "avoid broad, ambitious judicial rulings,"[88] seeking to say "no more than necessary to justify an outcome" while leaving "as much as possible undecided."[89] The goal is to obtain decisions with widespread public consensus; minimalists "prefer outcomes and opinions that can attract support from people holding many different theoretical positions."[90] As Posner has observed, this emphasis on narrowness aligns with pragmatism's proper "skepticism about various kinds of theorizing, including…constitutional theorizing."[91]

At first blush, minimalism appears to encourage caution and restraint. After all, Sunstein exhorts judges to say as little as possible in order to leave plenty of breathing room for the elected branches.[92] Moreover, the theory goes out of its way to be apolitical; Sunstein proudly proclaims that minimalism "does not dictate particular results"[93] and cannot be "easily characterized as 'liberal' or 'conservative.'"[94] His approach thus echoes many of the same values that judicial restraint seeks to vindicate; encouraging judges to avoid the political thicket enhances the legitimacy of their rulings.

In practice, however, minimalism is no barrier at all to judicial activism. Rather than condemn some of the most policy-driven decisions of the last century, Sunstein embraces them. For example, he hails both *Griswold* and *Heller* as minimalist because they took "small steps" and "narrowly focused on the particular provision[s] at issue."[95] This approach is misguided. Declaring new constitutional rights is one of the most consequential endeavors a court can undertake, no matter how prudently plotted the maiden voyage may appear to be. *Griswold* was in many ways a warm-up exercise for *Roe v. Wade*, and *Heller* was anything but the short step Sunstein would have us believe. In any event, to laud courts for slowly revolutionizing the Constitution misses the point. Here Posner is right to warn against the risks of such "wedge decisions, in which the Court takes a first tentative step toward a new abyss."[96]

Sunstein's response is to assert that the right to marital intimacy and the right to bear arms were not particularly objectionable, as "citizens and politicians of both parties" recognized their import.[97] That has it backwards. It is precisely when there is national consensus that judicial rights declaration is least necessary; to the extent such agreement exists, there is little reason to think the legislature won't respect it. And of course, when such consensus is absent, judicial involvement should be a last resort. Thus, while Sunstein himself characterizes minimalism as no "ordinary form" of judicial restraint, the truth is that as he applies it, it is no form at all.[98] While minimalism encourages judges to be modest in their tone and prose, it at most slows but does not stop them from taking the law wherever they see fit. As Posner himself describes it, minimalism is "a stealthy advance, by imperceptible steps, to Nirvana, liberal or conservative depending on the Justice's political ideology."[99] Taking shorter steps may lengthen the journey, but it does not change the destination.

Posner ultimately recognizes the risks of any kinship with Sunstein. He notes that "[a]lthough Sunstein's and [his] approaches are similar, [they] frequently disagree at the level of application to particular cases."[100] Moreover, Posner argues that Sunstein's theory is more result-oriented than his: while Sunstein "ha[s] a clear sense of where the nation, and the Supreme Court in the vanguard, should be heading," Posner's theory does not preordain the decision in any case. But considering Posner's own observations that a pragmatic judge should "come up with the decision that will be best with regard to present and future needs" and that "precedent, statutes, and constitutional text... [should be] limited constraints on his freedom of decision," it is hard to understand how Posner's theory provides more meaningful constraints on judicial discretion.[101] Put differently, Posner's pragmatism may differ from Sunstein's in the political valence of its outcomes, but both approaches invite judges to a policy roundtable where wisdom is the coin of the realm, not restraint.

Is Pragmatism the Last Man Standing?

Posner argues that even if pragmatism is activist, we have in the end no other choice: our methods of judicial selection, common law tradition, complex legal system, and unsuccessful constitutional theories "create an immense irreducible domain of discretionary lawmaking."[102] By looking at the consequences in these otherwise hopeless situations, "the judge is at least dealing with something that matters, and he can hope to make some progress and reduce error. Moreover, he is facilitating error-correction by not hiding behind a claim to possess an arcane methodology impenetrable to 'mere' policymakers and other noninitiates."[103]

Posner also argues we can correct for some of pragmatism's possible pitfalls with second-order solutions. We can carefully scrutinize judicial candidates to make sure that their policy preferences do not diverge too far from the mainstream and will roughly track majoritarian preferences.[104] We can also seek diversity. Posner argues that our implicit assumption that every judge should be of a certain sort— "empathetic or legalistic, activist or restrained, liberal or conservative"— is false. "[W]hat we really need is (within limits) a variety of types of judges, if we are to have any confidence in the robustness of judge-made law."[105] The advantages of pragmatism in legally unconstrained cases and the second-order solutions that can correct pragmatism's possible defects make pragmatism in Posner's view the only attractive option after all other cosmic constitutional theories have faltered.

I do agree with Posner that the cosmic constitutional theories are all ultimately unconvincing. But this is hardly enough to suggest we should embrace pragmatism by default. It's true that a pragmatist judge is dealing with things "that matter," but that cuts both ways;

judges are more likely to make mistakes when regulating air pollution, redistributing wealth, or improving race relations than interpreting statutes and precedents through more traditional approaches, the tasks for which their legal careers have prepared them. Even if traditional approaches fail to dictate a result, focusing intensely on such methods would be better than giving judges the heady view of their place and capabilities that pragmatism implies.

As with other cosmic theories, pragmatism hands judges their heady role in seductive terms. Judges are told to be pragmatic, not ideological. Pragmatism even has a certain restrained ring. Therein lies the problem. Cosmic theories blind judges because they are too grandiose. Pragmatism seduces judges by being much too casual. Formality of doctrine and the high church rituals of the law are among the sacraments that separate it from politics. If judges bow at the altar of text and structure, that is not all bad. There is no way to play up looking at the consequences and data without downplaying the formal rules and requirements of the interpretive task. One necessarily comes at the expense of another. By cutting away at traditional legal reasoning, pragmatism leaves judges in a worse place than it found them.

Perhaps in acknowledgment of pragmatism's activist weaknesses, Posner poses a troubling question: Is restraint worth it? Along these lines, he frequently defends Holmes's unofficial "puke" test, under which "a law was constitutional unless it made him want to 'puke.' "[106] Posner recognizes the "shapelessness," "subjectivity," "noncognitivism," "relativism," and "foundationlessness" of this approach.[107] But he argues that it is the only way judges will be able to get at laws like the anticontraception statute at issue in *Griswold v. Connecticut*.[108] The law there was "sectarian in motive and rationale, capriciously enforced, out of step with dominant public opinion in the country, genuinely oppressive, and…a national embarrassment." "It is not the worst thing in the world to have judges who are willing to strike down such laws in the name of the Constitution."[109] Similarly, a more straightforwardly pragmatic approach is justifiable, says Posner, even if it results in a kind of activism:

> [A]t their best, American appellate courts are councils of wise elders and it is not completely insane to entrust them with responsibility for deciding cases in a way that will produce the best results in the circumstances rather than just deciding cases in accordance with rules created by other organs of government or in accordance with their own previous decisions, although that is what they will be doing most of the time.[110]

The choice of words here is unfortunate. Constitutional review of the Holmesian variety is systematically less aggressive than the "council of wise elders" envisioned under the archetypically pragmatic approach. History and common sense suggest that grossly indigestible legislative outcomes will be rare and that courts will be reluctant to use this amorphous ground in exercising their most controversial power. A pragmatic approach, though, finds plenty of targets. Legislative outcomes rarely merit universal pragmatic acclaim—indeed, the opposite—and perhaps rightly so, as legislators must consider many factors other than the kinds of studies and interests a pragmatic judge may choose to balance. We once considered a Council of Revision that would have served a similar function to Judge Posner's Council of Wise Elders. Having rightly rejected that option at the front door long ago, we cannot let it in through the back door under the guise of an inescapable, beneficial pragmatism.

It seems in the end that Judge Posner is a victim of his own agile and wide-ranging intellect. One can respect this highly gifted man while doubting that the best and brightest among us can figure it all out. And to be fair, Judge Posner is half right. He's right that judging has always had, and will always have, an irreducible human component involving background, experience, and good judgment. He's right that the growing profusion of constitutional theories have failed at the laudable but elusive task of disciplining constitutional law. And he's right that given these facts, judges should keep an eye on consequences to ensure that in the exercise of their authority they do not blindly lead the blind into the ditch.

But a thoroughgoing pragmatism only exacerbates the problems remaining after we recognize the failure of other constitutional theories. To their credit, some of those theories at least purport to tether judges to something beyond preferences and balancing. Originalism puts heavy emphasis on constitutional text and history, traditional legal materials whose democratic imprimatur cannot be questioned if properly discerned and relevantly applied. And political process theory asks the judge to focus on the basis of our entire constitutional project, assertedly creating a legal order within which majorities have much room to determine their own fate while protecting minorities from their caprice. Black's pure textualism, while simplistic and one-dimensional, rightly emphasizes those words and phrases that have surmounted immense obstacles to become enshrined in our founding law.

These tethers have each proved to be a grand mirage. But pragmatism provides no tether at all. Part of the problem is the term itself, which invites judges to cast aside restraint whenever practical exigencies suggest that they do so. At best, pragmatism provides only a mood, a "sermon" against "theoretical pretentiousness" that cannot solve our legal problems and that pragmatism itself should be more careful to heed.[111] In explicitly rejecting any duty to the past and giving judges a vague instruction to seek optimal future outcomes, it simply sets the judge loose from the law. Although cosmic constitutional theories have faltered badly, the appropriate response is restraint, not adding fuel to the fire by giving judges a general charge to improve the world despite their lack of time, capacity, or authority to do so.

CHAPTER FIVE

. . .

The Failure of Cosmic Constitutional Theory

NOWHERE DOES THE Constitution mention judicial restraint. Nowhere does it say in so many words that judges shall duly hold themselves in check. In fact, the explicit wording of Article III may be argued to encourage the opposite. It provides that judges shall hold their offices "during good Behaviour," i.e., for life; that their compensation "shall not be diminished during their Continuance in Office"; and that their "Power shall extend" to certain important categories of cases. Someone reading Article III could be pardoned for thinking that judicial independence and authority were the Constitution's principal values, not judicial restraint.

The problem with this view, of course, is that Article III cannot be read in isolation. And when one compares its sparse nature to the copious grants of authority to the legislature and executive in Articles I and II, a sense of proportion must quickly take hold. Article III is not only shorter than Articles I and II. It follows them. Perhaps most importantly, the grants of power to the other branches of government are positive enumerations, none of which appear in

Article III. The grants leave no doubt that the powers of the legislature and executive call for active initiation, while the power of the courts is passively framed. The judges are not to reach out but to decide issues "only as litigation may spring up,"[1] with the personnel and under the rules and structures that the other branches of government have largely established.

It would thus take an extreme blindness not to discern that judicial restraint is a bedrock principle of America's founding and that the faith of the Framers lay at the end of the day with the organs of government more proximate to the people. And yet the power and endurance of the notion of restraint rests on something even beyond the functional layout of our founding document. That something is the premise of republican governance that authority be guided by more than mere appetite, the corollary being that those less fettered by such formal restraints as periodic elections must feel more constrained to hold themselves in check. That "activism" through the years has been such a term of opprobrium owes to the fact that it brings to mind a self-indulgence on the part of judges that citizens are quick to discern and loathe to approve.

It takes no cosmic constitutional theory to explain or justify this principle. The fact that judicial restraint is so often spoken of as *judicial self-restraint* indicates that judges are expected to shun hubris on their own. Nor is the demand for self-restraint a novel plea of the uninitiated. As Justice Powell noted, "Throughout our history, Justices of this Court have . . . admonish[ed] the nine . . . who sit on this bench of the duty of self-restraint."[2] This trait of self-denial is the furthest thing from being theoretical. It is an inner sense that judges must come to recognize as the essence of their calling.

The reasons for restraint have remained remarkably consistent and deceptively simple over time. One set of reasons speaks to the nature of judges themselves. We are not elected and hence not accountable to the people. In fact, the dispassionate ideals of our calling require us to be removed from the people, not wholly cloistered to be sure, but somewhat apart. Add to this distance the drawbacks of unrepresentativeness. Judges are drawn from the elite rungs of an elite profession. The picture of the robed and remote figures of the law interpreting law's mandates is one thing, but when the task of interpretation shades into imposition, the whole diverse collection of trades and callings in this country must naturally ask itself when and whether it consented to be ruled by only one.

When priests forsake their raiments, shall we listen to them then? When firemen leave behind their trucks and hoses, shall we listen to them then? When plumbers cease to talk of pipes and drains, shall we listen to them then? When judges lay aside the law for policy, shall we listen to them then? Of course we shall listen, as one citizen to another, but professions that leave behind their special province divest themselves not just of training and experience but of authority and legitimacy, and ultimately of social acceptance as well. What is left is brute power, not in the sense of guns and bayonets but in the more insidious respect that we do this because we can.

A second set of reasons for restraint owes to the nature not of judges but of constitutional adjudication. One may subscribe fully to the need and necessity of judicial review and yet recognize that the club of unconstitutionality is a weapon of last resort, precisely because it so often knocks every other player out of the ring. The declaration of rights so essential to liberty can ironically pose the greatest challenge to liberty when power is removed from Congress, the executive, the states, and ultimately the people by the thinnest of judicial margins. Whether five-to-four disablements of democratic majorities are more suspect than unanimous rulings may be open to debate, but surely the power to invoke the awesome majesty of the Constitution in the cause of far-flung yet uncertain consequences calls for a spirit of utmost sobriety in courts—"the spirit which is not too sure that it is right."[3] For while legislative majorities and states and even agencies can monitor their actions and revisit their mistakes, constitutional "[r]evisions cannot be made in the light of further experience"[4] unless and until the courts themselves come to concede or recognize their errors, something that human nature does not always find the wherewithal to do. So to supplant the diverse voices of an infinitely pluralistic people with one true and only word is an act whose enormity should never fail to register.

The more promiscuous forms of constitutional adjudication threaten to fracture the American social compact in the most elemental way. Power is ceded by the people to the state, not for purposes of aggrandizement, but in the spirit of republican virtue. That spirit long predates George Washington's renunciation of monarchical pretensions, as when the consul Cincinnatus, having saved Rome from the Aequi and the Volscians, relinquished his titles and returned to his farm. The placement of the admonition "No Title of Nobility shall be granted by the United States" in Article I can hardly be reason to suppose that the republican spirit should pass the Article III judiciary by. In fact, the trappings and deference enjoyed by aristocracies of all ages attach most readily to courts, and it is those inside our own marble palaces and gilded chambers who should resist the separation from that republican spirit that gave the nation birth, lest the courts indeed become "an oligarchic or aristocratic excrescence on our Constitution."[5] The advent of the imperial presidency does not supply the rationale for an imperial judiciary, for it is one thing for courts to check the excess of another and something else for us to superintend the ever more volatile subjects of democratic disputation with rulings designed to please our preferences.

The republican virtue of restraint requires no cosmic theory. For those content to respect the role of others in our constitutional system, no theory is needed. And all the theory in the world will not constrain judges bent on finding creative paths toward pleasing results. What is needed is a renewed recognition that it "is the essence of judicial duty to subordinate our own personal views"[6] and therefore for each side in the judicial wars to give something up. "America the Beautiful" is only a song, but several lines belong in Article III: "Confirm thy soul in self-control, / Thy liberty in law." Our self-control will be put to the test. The health care reform act of 2010 seems misconceived in many ways, but flawed legislation is not on that account unconstitutional. Similarly, same-sex marriage seems an inclusive and humane step, but the question remains whether courts have any business ordering it.

The controversies that flare brightly today provide no more than a glimmer of greater controversy tomorrow. The more volatile the issue, the less justification there often is for constitutionalizing it. Restraint is only restraint when we reject what we want most. For conservatives, this means that gun rights and property rights not ride so high in the saddle, impervious to democratic claims of public safety or environmental progress. For liberals, it means that unenumerated rights of choice not reign free of the need to accommodate conflicting moral and communal values that society has long been thought entitled to embody in the given law.

The sad thing is that merely to state such concessions is to condemn them, so acclimated are we to the thought that our most passionate beliefs must somehow be the subject of constitutional command. But to continue down this road is to cede our lives to judges. Liberty is both personal and democratic; when it dies "in the hearts of men and women . . . no constitution, no law, no court can save it."[7] And the courts that guarantee the historic rights of speech and religious exercise and the traditional freedoms from summary detention and restraint were never meant to preempt the people's prerogatives to self-governance and to harbor those inevitable plaintiffs of all imaginable persuasions whom democratic outcomes fail to suit.

It may perhaps be protested that the exercise of self-restraint leaves the Third Branch with no meaningful role to play and the judges themselves with rather little to do. But interpreting as opposed to making law is itself a difficult and time-consuming enterprise, and the protection of those constitutional rights unambiguously committed to our care remains "a great and stately jurisdiction." It is true enough that demonstrating deference and restraint will make our role less splashy, but it is that very contrast with celebrity culture that will lend the courts their stature and priceless independence, which is "the best preservative of the constitution."[8] And if one object of judicial authority is to provide stability and continuity to a society swept up in rapid change, then the practice of restraint would seem to serve that end.

I acknowledge, of course, that restraint is not an all-or-nothing matter. No judge is robotic, and where law commands intervention, it would transgress our oath to do otherwise. In fact, some of the greatest judicial proponents of restraint have had their activist moments, and often rightly so. The unanimous Court that invalidated the National Industrial Recovery Act included Justices Brandeis, Stone, and Cardozo,[9] whose commitment to constitutional restraint with regard to New Deal legislation was not seriously in question.[10] The unanimous Court that decided *Brown v. Board of Education* had as a member Justice Felix Frankfurter, whose commitment to restraint was, if anything, too severe.[11] One of the great practitioners of deference, the second Justice John Marshall Harlan,[12] found some legislative exercises, such as a ban on contraceptives in the marital bedroom, too extreme for his liking.[13] Justice Lewis Powell, whose career was governed by canons of caution, nonetheless voted with the majority in *Roe v. Wade*. Then too the supposedly nonactivist Rehnquist Court limited Congress's powers under the commerce clause[14] and Section 5 of the Fourteenth Amendment,[15] though such interventions hardly penetrated the core of legislative prerogative and had the beneficial effect of enhancing the democratic process in the several states. So to say that restraint is no inflexible command and that hard cases will, of course, continue to arise is not to countenance the routine aggressions of contemporary courts or the cosmic theories that have done so much to encourage them.

There exists the temptation to engage in nostalgia for some Golden Age of Restraint that never was. There have, to be sure, been individual justices (Holmes, Brandeis, Frankfurter, Harlan, and Powell among them) who took the habit of deference seriously. Their examples show that one can be a great justice without expounding a grand theory. While Harlan, for example, sought to preserve our federal structure by limiting the reach of the Fourteenth Amendment's due process clause to infringements of rights "implicit in the concept of ordered liberty,"[16] he did not spin that perspective into a grand theoretical web. The same is true for Brandeis and Powell, who were able to express inclinations about how to decide cases without claiming to have uncovered the Constitution's Rosetta Stone.[17] But even for these justices, it was unclear whether restraint correlated with self-denial; Brandeis, for example, "fervently believed in the economic justice of the legislation he voted to uphold."[18] More important, Brandeis, Harlan, and Powell, for all their talent, were unable to make of restraint a prevalent and enduring creed. By and large, self-restraint has waged a running battle with activist tendencies on the bench for more than a century, with the latter, albeit haltingly, more ascendant over time.

It is true, of course, that *Lochner* and its progeny gave interventions into economic regulation a bad name. But that setback to judicial expansionism was limited and temporary. A new form of intervention arose, this one focused on civil rights and liberties.

Major activist decisions of the Warren Court—*Brown v. Board of Education*,[19] *Gideon v. Wainwright*,[20] *Reynolds v. Sims*,[21] and *Miranda v. Arizona*[22]—have rightly stood the test of time, and that success doubtless strengthens the belief of today's interventionists that tomorrow may smile on their bolder efforts too.

They are wrong. Decisions like *Brown*, *Gideon*, and *Miranda* represent success stories because they vindicated foundational principles essential to the functioning of our nation. But I doubt there are now *Browns* and *Gideons* waiting to be born. One can debate the precise reach of eminent domain[23] or regulatory takings[24] or the value of same-sex marriage or the utility of firearms regulation[25] without believing that our Constitution is bereft of meaning if one's own beliefs are not embodied there. Those who wish to insert the courts into such contestable disputes would do well to remember that even the near misses of judicial activism expose its true dangers.[26] And the inestimable harm to our constitutional structure is not just the harm of bad decisions but the notion that judges should leave no frontiers of social policy unexplored.

Surely today's jurists recognize that the history is more complicated than *Brown*'s remarkable success might lead us to believe. Let us stipulate that *Roe v. Wade*,[27] *Swann v. Charlotte-Mecklenburg Board of Education*,[28] and *Boumediene v. Bush*,[29] for example, are not wrong decisions because they aroused strong passions. *Roe* was not wrong because it trampled on the moral and religious beliefs of countless numbers of Americans, but because it did so without foundation in constitutional text and history. *Swann* was not suspect because student transportation mandates strained middle-class allegiance and commitment to public education, but because it gave federal courts the broadest equitable powers over local school districts in contravention of every constitutional model of dual sovereignty.[30] *Boumediene*, which afforded greater habeas corpus access to Guantanamo detainees, was not problematic because of its opponents' fulminations on the war on terror, but because it encroached on the diplomatic and military options of the executive and the initiatives of Congress[31] with dubious regard for the Constitution's allocation of authority.

I appreciate the fact that many good and able people applaud one or more of these decisions, and I am grateful for their views. I understand that thoughtful minds may hail *Roe* as a triumph of living constitutionalism, *Swann* as a paradigm of we-they solicitude, and *Boumediene* as process theory at its best. But whatever their rightness or wrongness as matters of theory, those rulings are highly contestable as matters of law. And it should dawn upon us all that the risk of grave miscalculations affecting masses of Americans must rest on more than shallow legal premises. So while some Warren Court landmarks rightfully inspire, the notion that judicial activism from *Dred Scott* to the present has been an unalloyed *marche de triomphe* should not be placed before anyone with even the slightest ounce of skepticism. The many counterexamples that refute the case for activism should refute as well the cosmic theories that enable it.

Despite all this, the tradition of self-restraint persists, invoked stirringly by all sides.[32] Perhaps, however, it is not undue optimism to think that the appeal of self-restraint is more than tactical, that it bespeaks both modesty as to one's own views and respect for the opinions and judgments of others, that quality without which personal relations and communal peace and progress run aground. In leaving questions to democratic processes, courts convey the impression that Americans are in this together, that our destinies are interwoven, that our civic participation, however small, retains something of meaning and will not in the end be upstaged by the judicial will. In the timeless words of Learned Hand:

> For myself it would be most irksome to be ruled by a bevy of Platonic Guardians, even if I knew how to choose them, which I assuredly do not. If they were in charge, I should miss the

stimulus of living in a society where I have, at least theoretically, some part in the direction of public affairs. Of course I know how illusory would be the belief that my vote determined anything; but nevertheless when I go to the polls I have a satisfaction in the sense that we are all engaged in a common venture.[33]

It can be argued that as modern government grows ever larger, the courts must do likewise if the excesses of public bureaucracy are to be kept in check.[34] This argument fails, however, to see the judiciary as a bureaucratic system of its own, increasing not only in size but in the potential for intrusion. Judges are needed, and litigation is to some extent a necessity, but constant litigation can be a debilitating force, leading through countless delays, coercive process, and minutely fashioned orders to the very incursions on liberty against which the Third Branch was supposed to protect. Self-restraint is potentially an antidote to such behavior. But in shortchanging restraint, the cosmic theories have led us to overlook our own shortcomings.

Today there are few surprises. More often than not, if someone says that a given result was reached by a vote of five to four, the listener can name the five and the four. This has been true for some time. The Four Horseman on the New Deal Court were called that for a reason,[35] just as the trio of Brennan, Douglas, and Marshall tripped off the tongue for a reason too. What seems different now is not that certain justices vote together frequently, for that is hardly surprising, but that the lineups no longer coalesce around the historic dividing line of activism and restraint. In other words, justices of all persuasions can appear to migrate between activism and restraint depending on their personal beliefs. "And why do all of the justices so often find in the Constitution a mirror image of their own political and policy views on issues as diverse as abortion, race, religion, gay rights, campaign finance, the death penalty and national security?"[36] Whatever the explanation, it seems clear that cosmic theory has helped to spawn, or at least has done little to restrain, constitutional interventionism that is startling in both frequency and degree, and widely practiced on all sides.

Indeed, I fear that democratic liberty will more and more become the victim of cosmic theory's triumphal rise. The grand quest of the theorists has left restraint by the wayside and placed the inalienable right of Americans to self-governance at unprecedented risk. The increasing willingness of leading thinkers in the law to claim that their theory of the Constitution provides the answers has made citizens all the more willing to look to the courts to resolve the great social controversies of our time. In turn, the courts' eagerness to resolve such debates has cast them in a decidedly political light, making judicial selections and confirmation battles all the more disputatious. This state of affairs is exactly backwards. In a democracy, courts protect individual rights and personal liberties, but they are not, and should not be, the primary agents of social change. It is the people at the ballot box who should decide, not the people wearing black robes—the many, not the few.

Not all activism is equal. Some landmark decisions stray far more from constitutional text and from traditional subjects of judicial competence than others. Similarly, not all theories are equal. Some make far more of an effort to rein in runaway judicial rulings than others. But notwithstanding the valiant efforts to capture the American constitution in transcendent theory, no one can now plausibly make the claim that judging is impersonal, that constitutional rulings are dispassionate, or that decisions exhibit a respect for the bedrock principles of constitutional restraint even close to what the Framers envisioned or what the spirit of self-governance requires.

"But look, Judge Wilkinson, you can only beat a theory with a theory. So where's yours?" It's a fair question, but one that reveals, alas, how thoroughly theory has captured the modern constitutional mind. It's funny how few thought to pop that question to Powell, Harlan, Brandeis, or Holmes. Perhaps back then it was sufficient to note simply that restraint enhanced simultaneously the stature of the lawmaker and the judge. Perhaps it was sufficient to leave good judging to the presumptions of restraint and the particulars of the case.

Still, I have been tempted from time to time to develop a theory of my own, partly because it's just more fun to have a brightly colored banner to fly, and partly because the leading theories do have their virtues. But in rolling out a theory, I would be succumbing to many of the same grievous ills that I have just extensively criticized. More importantly, the theoretical enterprise is so weighted against restraint that it presages for coming generations democracy's slow decline.

What's needed is not yet another theory but an escape from theorizing. Convinced that they possess prearticulated frameworks that dictate unassailable results, theory-driven judges and scholars have forgotten that wisdom lies simply in knowing the limits of one's knowledge, that good sense is more often displayed in collective and diverse settings than in a rarefied appellate atmosphere, and that the language, structure, and history of law serve best as mediums of restraint rather than excuses for intrusion.

Perhaps in this Age of Theory, that reply seems insufficient. So be it. The increasing scope and stakes of constitutional litigation have brought the demands for judicial legitimacy to fever pitch. Theory itself tells us that only theorizing can sate these demands. But by clothing activism of every stripe in such seductive garb, theory fosters the kind of judicial adventurism that called the legitimacy of the courts into question in the first place. Restrained judges may lack the cachet of inhabiting the handsome mansion of a theory, but their modesty might some day return some greater measure of governance to those to whom it rightly belongs.

So what is my theory? The answer is I have no theory. I offer only a set of worn and ordinary observations that have all been voiced many times before. There is nothing novel in the idea that judges should pay attention to the text, structure, and history of the Constitution and not go creating rights out of whole cloth. Or that judges should appreciate "otherness"—the other branches of government, the other sovereign that is state government, the other institutions, professions, and trades that comprise the private sector. Or that liberty is best safeguarded when the allocation of authority to those others is respected by the courts. There is nothing new in the thought that life tenure provides the occasion not for expanding power but for appreciating its limitations. There is nothing remarkable in believing the highest virtues of judging—and of life—are a measure of self-denial and restraint.

It is altogether conventional to note that liberty is best preserved under law and that law is something above and apart from the personal preferences of men and women on the bench. I could go on, but nothing I have to suggest qualifies as a theory, much less a seminal one. My only point is that the search for cosmic theory has caused us to forget some mundane and humdrum truths, and that future generations will not look kindly on the usurpations that pursuits of unattainable ends have brought about.

Notes

. . .

INTRODUCTION

1. John Keats, *Ode on a Grecian Urn*, in 2 THE NORTON ANTHOLOGY OF ENGLISH LITERATURE 822, 822 (M. H. Abrams ed., 5th ed. 1986).

2. *See, e.g.*, ROBERT H. BORK, THE TEMPTING OF AMERICA 141 (1990) ("One of the more entertaining features of the literature is that the revisionists regularly destroy one another's arguments and seem to agree only on the impossibility or undesirability of adherence to the Constitution's original meaning.").

3. Robert H. Bork, *Neutral Principles and Some First Amendment Problems*, 47 IND. L.J. 1, 1 (1971).

CHAPTER ONE

1. William H. Rehnquist, *The Notion of a Living Constitution*, 54 TEX. L. REV. 693, 693 (1976).

2. Thomas B. Colby & Peter J. Smith, *Living Originalism*, 59 DUKE L.J. 239, 263 n.119 (2009).

3. *See generally* SETH STERN & STEPHEN WERMIEL, JUSTICE BRENNAN: LIBERAL CHAMPION (2010).

4. William J. Brennan, Jr., *The Constitution of the United States: Contemporary Ratification*, 27 S. TEX. L. REV. 433 (1986) [hereinafter Brennan, *Contemporary Ratification*].

5. *Id.* at 438.

6. *See* William J. Brennan, Jr., *Reason, Passion, and "The Progress of the Law*," 10 CARDOZO L. REV. 3, 12 (1988) [hereinafter Brennan, *Progress of the Law*] ("'[A] constitution states or ought to state not rules for the passing hour, but principles for an expanding future. In so far as it deviates from that standard, and descends into details and particulars, it loses its flexibility.... [To be] true to its function, it [must] maintain[] its power of adaptation, its suppleness, its play.") (quoting BENJAMIN CARDOZO, THE NATURE OF THE JUDICIAL PROCESS 83–84 (1921)).

7. Brennan, *Contemporary Ratification*, *supra* note 4, at 438–39, 445; *see also* Planned Parenthood of S.E. Pa. v. Casey, 505 U.S. 833, 916 (1992) (Stevens, J., concurring in part and dissenting in part).

8. Brennan, *Contemporary Ratification*, *supra* note 4, at 435, 438.

9. *Id.* at 436. This opinion prevails among contemporary living constitutionalists. *See, e.g.*, Laurence H. Tribe & Michael C. Dorf, *Levels of Generality in the Definition of Rights*, 57 U. CHI. L. REV. 1057, 1062–63 (1990) ("Originalism, however, cannot eliminate judges' need to appeal to extra-textual values because any inquiry into 'intent' must be indeterminate. Whose intent matters and at what level of generality? No judge can answer this question without reference to a value-laden, extra-textual political theory.").

10. Brennan, *Contemporary Ratification*, *supra* note 4, at 434–35.

11. DAVID A. STRAUSS, THE LIVING CONSTITUTION 36 (2010); *see also* Brennan, *Contemporary Ratification*, *supra* note 4, at 438 ("Current Justices read the Constitution in the only way that we can: as twentieth-century Americans.").

12. Antonin Scalia, *Originalism: The Lesser Evil*, 57 U. CIN. L. REV. 849, 864 (1989).

13. *See, e.g.*, Gonzales v. Raich, 545 U.S. 1 (2005) (allowing federal regulation of homegrown cannabis); Wickard v. Filburn, 317 U.S. 111 (1942) (allowing federal regulation of homegrown wheat).

14. *See, e.g.*, Whitman v. Am. Trucking Ass'ns, 531 U.S. 457, 472 (2001) (upholding a delegation to the Environmental Protection Agency

guided by the criterion "to protect the public health"); Mistretta v. United States, 488 U.S. 361, 372 (1989) ("[O]ur jurisprudence has been driven by a practical understanding that in our increasingly complex society, replete with ever changing and more technical problems, Congress simply cannot do its job absent an ability to delegate power under broad general directives.").

15. *See, e.g.*, Lawrence v. Texas, 539 U.S. 558 (2003) (right to consensual sexual conduct); Roe v. Wade, 410 U.S. 113 (1973) (right to abortion).

16. STRAUSS, *supra* note 11, at 17.

17. Brennan, *Contemporary Ratification, supra* note 4, at 440.

18. David A. Strauss, *Common Law Constitutional Interpretation*, 63 U. CHI. L. REV. 877, 926–27 (1996).

19. *Id.* at 892–93.

20. STRAUSS, *supra* note 11, at 76.

21. *See supra* note 6.

22. Brennan, *Contemporary Ratification, supra* note 4, at 438, 440.

23. 347 U.S. 483 (1954).

24. See, for example, Michael Klarman's able study, FROM JIM CROW TO CIVIL RIGHTS (2004).

25. *See, e.g.*, Michael J. Klarman, *Brown, Originalism, and Constitutional Theory: A Response to Professor McConnell*, 81 VA. L. REV. 1881 (1995). *But see* Michael W. McConnell, *Originalism and the Desegregation Decisions*, 81 VA. L. REV. 947 (1995) (challenging the scholarly consensus that *Brown* could not be grounded in the historical understanding of the Fourteenth Amendment).

26. Brennan, *Contemporary Ratification, supra* note 4, at 437; *see also* Andrew B. Coan, *Talking Originalism*, 2009 BYU L. REV. 847, 853 ("The deck is so heavily stacked against amendment—and stacked not by us but by the very dead ancestors whose grip amendments are supposed to shrug off—that the Constitution is, in almost all important respects, frozen in its current form.").

27. *See* STRAUSS, *supra* note 11, at 78 ("Anyone who doubts that *Brown* is lawful is a fringe player, at best."); Richard A. Posner, *The Supreme Court, 2004 Term—Foreword: A Political Court*, 119 HARV. L. REV. 31, 48 (2005) (recognizing that "no responsible critic of the Court questions the soundness of *Brown* anymore").

28. Pub. L. No. 88-352, 78 Stat. 241 (1964).

29. *See, e.g.*, Brown v. Bd. of Educ. (*Brown II*), 349 U.S. 294, 301 (1955) (demanding desegregation "with all deliberate speed," but achieving somewhat less).

30. *See* Heart of Atlanta Motel, Inc. v. United States, 379 U.S. 241 (1964) (holding that Title II of the Civil Rights Act of 1964 fell within Congress's commerce clause authority); Katzenbach v. McClung, 379 U.S. 294 (1964) (same).

31. *See* Frontiero v. Richardson, 411 U.S. 677 (1973) (striking down an armed services policy that automatically provided benefits to dependent wives of servicemen but not to husbands of servicewomen).

32. *See* WALDO E. MARTIN, JR., BROWN V. BOARD OF EDUCATION: A BRIEF HISTORY WITH DOCUMENTS 34 (1998).

33. United States v. E. C. Knight Co., 156 U.S. 1 (1895); *see also* Hammer v. Dagenhart, 247 U.S. 251 (1918) (striking down child labor regulations as beyond Congress's commerce power).

34. *See, e.g.*, A.L.A. Schechter Poultry Corp. v. United States, 295 U.S. 495 (1935) (finding part of the National Industrial Recovery Act beyond Congress's commerce power); Carter v. Carter Coal Co., 298 U.S. 238 (1936) (finding parts of the Bituminous Coal Conservation Act beyond Congress's commerce power).

35. *See* NLRB v. Jones & Laughlin Steel Corp., 301 U.S. 1 (1937) (upholding the National Labor Relations Act); United States v. Darby, 312 U.S. 100 (1941) (upholding the Fair Labor Standards Act and overruling *Hammer v. Dagenhart*); *see also* cases cited *supra* note 30.

36. United States v. Lopez, 514 U.S. 549, 568 (1995) (Kennedy, J., concurring).

37. *See* Wickard v. Filburn, 317 U.S. 111, 127–28 (1942).

38. *See, e.g.*, Lopez, 514 U.S. at 556.

39. *See* Gonzales v. Raich, 545 U.S. 1 (2005); United States v. Morrison, 529 U.S. 598 (2000); *Lopez*, 514 U.S. 549.

40. Robert H. Bork, *Styles in Constitutional Theory*, 26 S. TEX. L.J. 383, 389 (1985).

41. *See* San Antonio Indep. Sch. Dist. v. Rodriguez, 411 U.S. 1, 70 (1973) (Marshall, J., dissenting) (public education); Dandridge v. Williams, 397 U.S. 471, 508 (1970) (Marshall, J., dissenting) (welfare benefits).

42. Roe v. Wade, 410 U.S. 113 (1973) (abortion); Griswold v. Connecticut, 381 U.S. 479 (1965) (contraceptives).

43. Brennan, *Contemporary Ratification, supra* note 4, at 439.

44. Trop v. Dulles, 356 U.S. 86, 101 (1958).

45. *See, e.g.*, Swann v. Charlotte-Mecklenburg Bd. of Educ., 402 U.S. 1 (1971).

46. Rehnquist, *supra* note 1, at 706.

47. *See* Antonin Scalia, *Common-Law Courts in a Civil-Law System: The Role of United States Federal Courts in Interpreting the Constitution and Laws, in* SCALIA, A MATTER OF INTERPRETATION: FEDERAL COURTS AND THE LAW 3, 40 (Amy Gutmann ed., 1997) ("If courts felt too much bound by the democratic process to tinker with statutes, when their tinkering could be adjusted by the legislature, how much more should they feel bound not to tinker with a constitution, when their tinkering is virtually irreparable.").

48. Steven G. Gey, *The Procedural Annihilation of Structural Rights*, 61 HASTINGS L.J. 1, 60 (2009).

49. *See* Brennan, *Contemporary Ratification, supra* at 444 (asserting that the justices "are the last word on the meaning of the Constitution"). Contemporary living constitutionalists often claim that their theories are not invitations to judicial exclusivity in constitutional interpretation. *See, e.g.*, RONALD DWORKIN, FREEDOM'S LAW: THE MORAL READING OF THE AMERICAN CONSTITUTION 12 (1996) ("The moral reading . . . is a theory about what the Constitution means, not a theory about whose view of what it means must be accepted by the rest of us."); STRAUSS, *supra*, at 48 ("It is, therefore, easy to imagine common law constitutionalism in a system without judicial review."). This claim, however, ignores the fact that when judicial review is so ingrained in the constitutional culture, judges are far more likely than elected officials to be constitutional theory's audience and to implement its prescriptions. And once judges have declared the scope of a right, neither the elected branches nor the states may define that right more narrowly.

50. *See* Abraham Lincoln, *First Inaugural Address (Mar. 4, 1861), in* ABRAHAM LINCOLN: HIS SPEECHES AND WRITINGS 579, 585–86 (Roy P. Basler ed., 1976) ("[I]f the policy of the government upon vital questions affecting the whole people is to be irrevocably fixed by decisions of the Supreme Court . . . , the people will have ceased to be their own rulers, having to that extent practically resigned their government into the hands of that eminent tribunal.").

51. GOODWIN LIU, PAMELA S. KARLAN & CHRISTOPHER H. SCHROEDER, KEEPING FAITH WITH THE CONSTITUTION 24 (2009).

52. *See* ADRIAN VERMEULE, LAW AND THE LIMITS OF REASON 11–12 (2009) (suggesting that the size, representativeness, and professional diversity of legislatures are significant advantages relative to courts for the interpretation of vague constitutional provisions).

53. *See* AKHIL REED AMAR, AMERICA'S CONSTITUTION 64–74 (2005) (describing the constitutional architecture for this broad representation).

54. Dennis v. United States, 341 U.S. 494, 525 (1951) (Frankfurter, J., concurring).

55. JOHN R. VILE, THE CONSTITUTIONAL CONVENTION OF 1787, 634 (2005) (quoting James Wilson of Pennsylvania on the power of the convention).

56. Brown v. Plata, 131 S. Ct. 1910, 1922(2011).

57. *Id.* at 1959 (Alito, J., dissenting).

58. Vieth v. Jubelirer, 541 U.S. 267, 305 (2004) (plurality); *see also* Planned Parenthood of S.E. Pa. v. Casey, 505 U.S. 833, 854–55 (1992) (plurality) (acknowledging that "the rule of *stare decisis* is not an inexorable command, and certainly it is not such in every constitutional case" but nonetheless maintaining the "central holding" of *Roe v. Wade*) (internal quotation omitted).

59. 428 U.S. 153 (1976).

60. *See, e.g.*, Gardner v. Florida, 430 U.S. 349, 364–65 (1977) (Brennan, J., dissenting in part) ("I adhere to my view that the death penalty is in all circumstances cruel and unusual punishment prohibited by the Eighth and Fourteenth Amendments.").

61. *Furman*, 408 U.S. at 269 (Brennan, J., concurring) (quoting Trop v. Dulles, 356 U.S. 86, 100–01 (1958)).

62. *See Gregg*, 428 U.S. at 179–80 (plurality).

63. Brennan, *Contemporary Ratification, supra* note 4, at 444 ("On this issue, the death penalty, I hope to embody a community, although perhaps not yet arrived."); *id.* ("This is an interpretation to which a majority of my fellow Justices—not to mention, it would seem, a majority of my fellow countrymen—does not subscribe."); *see also Gregg*, 428 U.S. at 227–31 (Brennan, J., dissenting) (resting his opposition on moral arguments rather than legislative consensus).

64. The quotations in this paragraph are from JAMES B. THAYER, JOHN MARSHALL 106–07 (1901).

65. Planned Parenthood of S.E. Pa. v. Casey, 505 U.S. 833, 1002 (1992) (Scalia, J., concurring in part and dissenting in part).

66. *See* Brennan, *Contemporary Ratification, supra* note 4, at 436 ("It is the very purpose of our Constitution . . . to declare certain values transcendent, beyond the reach of temporary political majorities.").

67. *See* Lochner v. New York, 198 U.S. 45 (1905); *see also id.* at 75 (Holmes, J., dissenting) ("I strongly believe that my agreement or disagreement has nothing to do with the right of a majority to embody their opinions in law.").

68. *See* Griswold v. Connecticut, 381 U.S. 479 (1965); Eisenstadt v. Baird, 405 U.S. 438 (1972); Roe v. Wade, 410 U.S. 113 (1973).

69. *But see* Pierce v. Soc'y of Sisters, 268 U.S. 510 (1925) (overturning on substantive due process grounds a state law requiring primary education at public schools); Meyer v. Nebraska, 262 U.S. 390 (1923) (similarly striking down a statute prohibiting foreign-language education).

70. 397 U.S. 471, 508 (1970) (Marshall, J., dissenting).

71. 405 U.S. 56, 81–83 (1972) (Douglas, J., dissenting).

72. 411 U.S. 1, 62–63 (1973) (Brennan, J., dissenting).

73. *See* San Antonio Indep. Sch. Dist. v. Rodriguez, 411 U.S. 1, 35 (1973) (Powell, J.) ("Education, of course, is not among the rights afforded explicit protection under our Federal Constitution. Nor do we find any basis for saying it is implicitly so protected."); Lindsey v. Normet, 405 U.S. at 74 (White, J.) ("We do not denigrate the importance of decent, safe, and sanitary housing. But the Constitution does not provide judicial remedies for every social and economic ill."); Dandridge v. Williams, 397 U.S. at 487 (Stewart, J.) ("[T]he intractable economic, social, and even philosophical problems presented by public welfare assistance programs are not the business of this Court.").

74. *See, e.g.,* Williams v. Taylor, 529 U.S. 362, 384–85 (2000) (Stevens, J.) ("In constitutional adjudication, as in the common law, rules of law often develop incrementally as earlier decisions are applied to new factual situations.").

75. Strauss, *supra* note 18, at 901–2; *see also id.* ("There is some moral (or policy, or fairness) component to many unsettled constitutional issues. . . . Moral or policy arguments can be sufficiently strong to outweigh those traditionalist concerns to some degree, and to the extent they do, traditionalism must give way.").

76. *Id.* at 914.

77. Justice David H. Souter, Speech at Harvard University Commencement (May 27, 2010) (transcript available at http://news.harvard.edu/gazette/story/2010/05/text-of-justice-david-souters-speech).

78. DWORKIN, *supra* note 49, at 2.

79. McDonald v. City of Chicago, 130 S. Ct. 3020, 3096 (2010) (Stevens, J., dissenting).

80. *See, e.g.,* Stenberg v. Carhart, 530 U.S. 914 (2000) (Breyer, J.) (announcing the holding of the Court that a Nebraska statute criminalizing partial birth abortion was unconstitutional).

81. *See* United States v. Morrison, 529 U.S. 598, 655 (2000) (Breyer, J., dissenting); United States v. Lopez, 514 U.S. 549, 615 (1995) (Breyer, J., dissenting).

82. *See* Van Orden v. Perry, 545 U.S. 677, 698 (2005) (Breyer, J., concurring).

83. *See McDonald,* 130 S. Ct. at 3120 (Breyer, J., dissenting); District of Columbia v. Heller, 554 U.S. 570, 681 (2008) (Breyer, J., dissenting).

84. *See* STEPHEN BREYER, ACTIVE LIBERTY: INTERPRETING OUR DEMOCRATIC CONSTITUTION 17 (2005).

85. *See, e.g.,* RICHARD A. EPSTEIN, TAKINGS: PRIVATE PROPERTY AND THE POWER OF EMINENT DOMAIN 279–80 (1985).

86. Brennan, *Progress of the Law, supra* note, at 8.

CHAPTER TWO

1. ROBERT H. BORK, THE TEMPTING OF AMERICA (1990). Judge Bork's articles offer additional insights into his theory. *See, e.g.,* Robert H. Bork, *Neutral Principles and Some First Amendment Problems,* 47 IND. L.J. 1, 1 (1971).

2. *See* Barron v. City of Baltimore, 32 U.S. (7 Pet.) 243, 250 (1833).

3. *See* Grant v. Raymond, 31 U.S. (6 Pet.) 218, 241 (1832).

4. *See* Cherokee Nation v. Georgia, 30 U.S. (5 Pet.) 1, 18 (1831).

5. *See* Gibbons v. Ogden, 22 U.S. (9 Wheat.) 1, 188 (1824).

6. *See* Cohens v. Virginia, 19 U.S. (6 Wheat.) 264, 416–17 (1821).

7. Marbury v. Madison, 5 U.S. (1 Cranch) 137, 179–80 (1803).

8. *See, e.g.,* Pamela S. Karlan, *Bullets, Ballots, and Battles on the Roberts Court,* 35 OHIO N.U. L. REV. 445, 449 (2008) (calling Black a "sort of patron

saint of textualism"); Mark Tushnet, *"Meet the New Boss": The New Judicial Center*, 83 N.C. L. Rev. 1205, 1208 (2005) ("Justice Hugo Black was a strict textualist.").

9. *See* Noah Feldman, Scorpions: The Battles and Triumphs of FDR's Great Supreme Court Justices 145 (2010).

10. Black's dissent in *Adamson v. California*, 332 U.S. 46 (1947), in which he argued that the original understanding of the Fourteenth Amendment made the Bill of Rights fully applicable to the states, is illustrative. *See Adamson*, 332 U.S. at 68–72 (Black, J., dissenting). Of course, these protean originalist sensibilities only highlight the ways in which Black was a precursor of Bork. *See* Feldman, *supra* note 9, at 145.

11. *See, e.g.*, Griswold v. Connecticut, 381 U.S. 479, 509 (1965) (Black, J., dissenting) ("I have expressed the view many times that First Amendment freedoms, for example, have suffered from a failure of the courts to stick to the simple language of the First Amendment in construing it, instead of invoking multitudes of words substituted for those the Framers used."); Hugo L. Black, *The Bill of Rights*, 35 N.Y.U. L. Rev. 865, 874 (1960) ("The phrase 'Congress shall make no law' is composed of plain words, easily understood.").

12. *Griswold*, 381 U.S. at 507–08.

13. Feldman, *supra* note 9, at 346.

14. *See, e.g.*, Steven G. Calabresi, *"A Shining City on a Hill": American Exceptionalism and the Supreme Court's Practice of Relying on Foreign Law*, 86 B.U. L. Rev. 1335, 1400 (2006); William W. Van Alstyne, *Reflections on the Teaching of Constitutional Law*, 49 St. Louis U. L.J. 653, 658 n.16 (2005).

15. *Griswold*, 381 U.S. at 520.

16. *Id.* at 525–26 (quoting Adamson v. California, 332 U.S. 46, 90–92 (1947) (Black, J., dissenting)).

17. *Id.* at 513; *see also* Conn. Gen. Life Ins. Co. v. Johnson, 303 U.S. 77, 85 (1938) (Black, J., dissenting) (arguing that a California corporate tax did not violate the due process clause of the Fourteenth Amendment based on Black's belief that "the word 'person' in the Fourteenth Amendment [does not] include[] corporations"); John F. Manning, *What Divides Textualists from Purposivists?*, 106 Colum. L. Rev. 70, 76 (2006) (arguing that textualism does not allow "pressing policy cues" to overcome "semantic evidence").

18. *See infra* notes 39–51 and accompanying text.

19. U.S. CONST. amend. I.

20. *See* United States v. O'Brien, 391 U.S. 367 (1968) (upholding conviction for burning Selective Service registration certificate as part of Vietnam War protest).

21. *See* Nicholas Quinn Rosenkranz, *The Subjects of the Constitution*, 62 STAN. L. REV. 1209, 1271 & n.246 (2010) ("[T]he word 'association' does not appear in the First Amendment."). Yet Black joined the Court's opinion in *NAACP v. Alabama ex rel. Patterson*, 357 U.S. 449, 460 (1963), which declared that freedom of association "is an inseparable aspect of the 'liberty' assured by the Due Process Clause of the Fourteenth Amendment, which embraces freedom of speech."

22. JOHN HART ELY, DEMOCRACY AND DISTRUST 13 (1980).

23. *See, e.g.,* Dandridge v. Williams, 397 U.S. 471, 528–29 (1970) (Marshall, J., dissenting).

24. *See, e.g.,* Home Bldg. & Loan Ass'n v. Blaisdell, 290 U.S. 398, 473 (1934) (Sutherland, J., dissenting).

25. *See* BORK, *supra* note 1, at 69–70.

26. *Id.* at 143 ("In truth, only the approach of original understanding meets the criteria that any theory of constitutional adjudication must meet in order to possess democratic legitimacy.").

27. *Id.* at 139–40.

28. *Id.* at 140–41.

29. *Id.* at 145–46.

30. Herbert Wechsler, *Toward Neutral Principles of Constitutional Law*, 73 HARV. L. REV. 1, 19 (1959).

31. BORK, *supra* note 1, at 146.

32. *Id.* at 146, 149, 151.

33. *Id.* at 144.

34. *Id.* at 143–45, 162–63.

35. *Id.* at 158.

36. *Id.* at 151.

37. Robert H. Bork, *The Constitution, Original Intent, and Economic Rights*, 23 SAN DIEGO L. REV. 823, 826–27 (1986).

38. BORK, *supra* note 1, at 163–64.

39. *Id.* at 153.

40. *See* Michael W. McConnell, *Active Liberty: A Progressive Alternative to Textualism and Originalism?*, 119 HARV. L. REV. 2387, 2414 (2006)

(reviewing STEPHEN BREYER, ACTIVE LIBERTY: INTERPRETING OUR DEMOCRATIC CONSTITUTION (2005)).

41. U.S. CONST. art. II, § 1, cl. 5.

42. U.S. CONST. art. I, § 8, cl. 7.

43. *See* 521 U.S. 702, 710–19 (1997).

44. *See* Compassion in Dying v. Washington, 79 F.3d 790 (9th Cir. 1996) (en banc), *rev'd sub nom.*, Washington v. Glucksberg, 521 U.S. 702 (1997).

45. *See* Antonin Scalia, *Originalism: The Lesser Evil*, 57 U. CIN. L. REV. 849, 863 (1989).

46. BORK, *supra* note 1, at 163.

47. *See* 381 U.S. 479 (1965).

48. BORK, *supra* note 1, at 151, 163.

49. *See* Scalia, *supra* note 45, at 849, 862–64.

50. BORK, *supra* note 1, at 163.

51. Scalia, *supra* note 45, at 863–64.

52. BORK, *supra* note 1, at 143.

53. *See id.* at 145–46 (explaining that judges must utilize external neutral principles in order to avoid becoming unelected tyrants).

54. *See id.* at 143 (noting that treating the Constitution as a source of law guarantees that it will have "a meaning independent of our own desires.").

55. *Id.* at 144–45.

56. Bork, *supra* note 37, at 826.

57. ELY, *supra* note 22, at 3.

58. BORK, *supra* note 1, at 144–45.

59. *Id.* at 139–40, 146.

60. *Id.* I say "in theory" because it would be irresponsible not to call attention to the fact that these claims of democratic legitimacy rest on the premises that originalism constrains judges and that it gives them the fortitude necessary to resist the temptations of judicial activism. As will be discussed below, these premises are very much in dispute.

61. *See id.* at 153–55.

62. *Id.* at 154. The Council of Revision proposal would have placed veto power in a council consisting of the executive and a number of federal judges. *Id.*

63. To be fair, the historical evidence on the point is in dispute. *See, e.g.*, H. Jefferson Powell, *The Original Understanding of Original Intent*, 98

Harv. L. Rev. 885, 948 (1985) ("It is commonly assumed that the 'interpretive intention' of the Constitution's framers was that the Constitution would be construed in accordance with what future interpreters could gather of the framers' own purposes, expectations, and intentions. Inquiry shows that assumption to be incorrect.").

64. Sanford Levinson, *The Limited Relevance of Originalism in the Actual Performance of Legal Roles*, 19 Harv. J.L. & Pub. Pol'y 495, 495 (1996).

65. *See id.*; *see also* Daniel A. Farber, *The Originalism Debate: A Guide for the Perplexed*, 49 Ohio St. L.J. 1085, 1086 (1989) ("Almost no one believes that the original understanding is wholly irrelevant to modern-day constitutional interpretation.").

66. Goodwin Liu, Pamela S. Karlan & Christopher H. Schroeder, Keeping Faith with the Constitution 35 (2009).

67. Breyer, *supra* note 40, at 7.

68. *See* McDonald v. Smith, 472 U.S. 479, 485–90 (1985) (Brennan, J., concurring) (analyzing the original understanding of the First Amendment).

69. *See* Mitchell N. Berman, *Originalism Is Bunk*, 84 N.Y.U. L. Rev. 1, 87 (2009).

70. 527 U.S. 706 (1999).

71. *See id.* at 712–54; *id.* at 761–808 (Souter, J., dissenting). The precise issue in *Alden* was whether "the powers delegated to Congress under Article I . . . include the power to subject nonconsenting States to private suits for damages in state courts." *Id.* at 712 (majority opinion).

72. *See* Berman, *supra* note 69, at 87.

73. Richard A. Posner, *Bork and Beethoven*, 42 Stan. L. Rev. 1365, 1378 (1990).

74. U.S. Term Limits, Inc. v. Thornton, 514 U.S. 779, 783 (1995).

75. *Id.* Article I, § 2, cl. 2 states, "No Person shall be a Representative who shall not have attained to the Age of twenty five Years, and been seven Years a Citizen of the United States, and who shall not, when elected, be an Inhabitant of that State in which he shall be chosen." Article I, § 3, cl. 3 states, "No Person shall be a Senator who shall not have attained to the Age of thirty Years, and been nine Years a Citizen of the United States, and who shall not, when elected, be an Inhabitant of that State for which he shall be chosen."

76. *See Thornton*, 515 U.S. at 787–838; *id.* at 845–916 (Thomas, J., dissenting); *see also* Gregory E. Maggs, *Which Original Meaning of the Consti-*

tution Matters to Justice Thomas?, 4 N.Y.U. J.L. & LIBERTY 494, 510–11 (2009) (explaining that the majority and dissent both engaged in originalist analysis in *Thornton* but came to opposite conclusions).

77. *Thornton*, 515 U.S. at 783 ("The Arkansas Supreme Court held that the [term limits] amendment violates the Federal Constitution. We agree with that holding."); *id.* at 845 (Thomas, J., dissenting) ("Nothing in the Constitution deprives the people of each State of the power to prescribe eligibility requirements for the candidates who seek to represent them in Congress.").

78. *See* Farber, *supra* note 65, at 1089.

79. *See* Vasan Kesavan & Michael Stokes Paulsen, *The Interpretive Force of the Constitution's Secret Drafting History*, 91 GEO. L.J. 1113, 1212–14 (2003) ("The statements of Framers are no less and no more important than the statements of Ratifiers; it is what the text means that counts, not what any particular body or group intended, expected, or understood. Subjective statements by Framers and Ratifiers are generally helpful in determining what the text means to the ordinary, reasonably well-informed hypothetical Ratifier."); Akhil Reed Amar, *Our Forgotten Constitution: A Bicentennial Comment*, 97 YALE L.J. 281, 288–89 (1987) ("In theory, records of the state ratifying conventions are better evidence than records from Philadelphia, because ratification debates by definition constitute popular and public history—history of, by, and for the People.").

80. *See Thornton*, 514 U.S. at 856 (Thomas, J., dissenting) ("Justice Story was a brilliant and accomplished man, and one cannot casually dismiss his views. On the other hand, he was not a member of the Founding generation, and his *Commentaries on the Constitution* were written a half century after the framing."); *see also* Maggs, *supra*, at 510–11 ("[Justice Thomas], like Justice Stevens, took an Originalist view of the issue [in *Thornton*] but was concerned with the weight that Stevens had given to Justice Story's treatise[,] [f]inding other evidence more persuasive....").

81. *See* District of Columbia v. Heller, 554 U.S. 570, 612–19 (2008) (noting evidence of the original understanding of the Second Amendment from the late nineteenth century).

82. William J. Brennan, Jr., *The Constitution of the United States: Contemporary Ratification*, 27 S. TEX. L. REV. 433, 435 (1986) [hereinafter Brennan, *Contemporary Ratification*].

83. BORK, *supra* note 1, at 165, 183.

84. *See, e.g.*, Doe v. Bolton, 410 U.S. 179, 210 (1973) (Douglas, J., concurring) ("The Ninth Amendment obviously does not create federally enforceable rights."); Griswold v. Connecticut, 381 U.S. 479, 488 (1965) (Goldberg, J., concurring) ("The language and history of the Ninth Amendment reveal that the Framers of the Constitution believed that there are additional fundamental rights, protected from governmental infringement, which exist alongside those fundamental rights specifically mentioned in the first eight constitutional amendments."); Randy E. Barnett, *The Ninth Amendment: It Means What It Says*, 85 TEX. L. REV. 1, 80 (2006) ("The Ninth Amendment prohibits constitutional constructions—like that propounded by the Supreme Court in Footnote Four of *Carolene Products*—that infringe upon the unenumerated, natural, and individual rights retained by the people. In other words, it means what it says.").

85. Brennan, *Contemporary Ratification, supra* note 82, at 435.

86. *See* McDonald v. City of Chicago, 130 S. Ct. 3020, 3063–88 (2010) (Thomas, J., concurring in part and in the judgment).

87. *See* The Slaughter-House Cases, 83 U.S. (16 Wall.) 36, 66–82 (1872) (contending that the privileges or immunities clause protects only a narrow set of rights).

88. *See McDonald*, 130 S. Ct. at 3063–83 (Thomas, J., concurring in part and in the judgment) (advocating a broad reading of the privileges or immunities clause).

89. *Compare id.* at 3028–31 (majority opinion) *and* The Slaughter-House Cases, 83 U.S. (16 Wall.) at 66–82, *with McDonald*, 130 S. Ct. at 3063–83 (Thomas, J., concurring in part and in the judgment).

90. BORK, *supra* note 1, at 166.

91. Brennan, *Contemporary Ratification, supra* note 82, at 435.

92. H. Jefferson Powell, *On Not Being "Not an Originalist,"* 7 U. ST. THOMAS L.J. 259, 274 (2010) ("Very few people likely to become judges have the training to do originalist work well and the adversarial process is not structured to provide courts with historical analysis that can be taken seriously—the mocking epithet 'law office history' is not a joke.").

93. *See* Richard A. Posner, *In Defense of Looseness: The Supreme Court and Gun Control*, THE NEW REPUBLIC, Aug. 27, 2008, at 32, 35 (describing the "law office history" that judges engage in, marshalling the historical evidence only on their side of the dispute).

94. DAVID A. STRAUSS, THE LIVING CONSTITUTION 19 (2010).

95. Scalia, *supra* note 45, at 860–61.

96. *See* Adamson v. California, 332 U.S. 46, 68 (1947) (Black, J., dissenting).

97. *See* Fay v. Noia, 372 U.S. 391 (1962) (Brennan, J.).

98. *See, e.g.*, Charles Fairman, *Does the Fourteenth Amendment Incorporate the Bill of Rights?* 2 Stan. L. Rev. 5, 139 (1949) ("In [Justice Black's] contention that Section I [of the Fourteenth Amendment] was intended and understood to impose Amendments I to VIII upon the states, the record of history is overwhelmingly against him."); Dallin H. Oaks, *Legal History in the High Court—Habeas Corpus*, 64 Mich. L. Rev. 451, 459 (1966) ("Legal historians—even those cited in the opinion—hold a view that is at odds with the historical analysis in the *Fay* case."); Lewis Mayers, *The Habeas Corpus Act of 1867: The Supreme Court as Legal Historian*, 33 U. Chi. L. Rev. 31, 58 (1965) ("[I]t seems clear that the Court's claim of merely fulfilling the intentions of the 1867 Congress is without historical foundation.").

99. *See, e.g.*, District of Columbia v. Heller, 554 U.S. 570 (2008); McDonald v. City of Chicago, 130 S. Ct. 3020 (2010).

100. William E. Nelson, *History and Neutrality in Constitutional Adjudication*, 72 Va. L. Rev. 1237, 1250–51 (1986).

101. *See, e.g.*, Regents of Univ. of Cal. v. Bakke, 438 U.S. 265, 291–93 (1978) (Powell, J.) ("Indeed, it is not unlikely that among the Framers were many who would have applauded a reading of the Equal Protection Clause that states a principle of universal application and is responsive to the racial, ethnic, and cultural diversity of the Nation.").

102. *See, e.g., id.* at 396–98 (Marshall, J., concurring) (arguing that the Fourteenth Amendment does not prohibit affirmative action because "[s]uch a result would pervert the intent of the Framers by substituting abstract equality for the genuine equality the Amendment was intended to achieve").

103. Bork, *supra* note 1, at 146–50.

104. Brown v. Entm't Merchs. Ass'n, 131 S. Ct. 2729 (2011).

105. *See* Robert Barnes, *What Would the Founders Do? Scalia and Thomas Disagree on Originalism*, Wash. Post, July 4, 2011, at A13.

106. Alexander M. Bickel, The Least Dangerous Branch 39 (1962).

107. Bork, *supra* note 1, at 151.

108. Scalia, *supra* note 45, at 861–62.

109. BORK, *supra* note 1, at 158.

110. Stuart Taylor Jr., *Why the Justices Play Politics*, WASH. POST, July 14, 2010, at A19.

111. Scalia, *supra* note 45, at 861.

112. 367 U.S. 643 (1961).

113. 377 U.S. 533 (1964).

114. 411 U.S. 677 (1973).

115. *See Frontiero*, 411 U.S. at 691–92 (Powell, J., concurring in judgment); *Reynolds*, 377 U.S. at 589–625 (Harlan, J., dissenting); *Mapp*, 367 U.S. at 672–86 (Harlan, J., dissenting).

116. For example, judges have limited the exclusionary rule, but they have left the basic rule intact. *See* Hudson v. Michigan, 547 U.S. 586 (2006) (holding that the exclusionary rule does not apply to a violation of the knock-and-announce requirement); United States v. Leon, 468 U.S. 897 (1984) (establishing the good faith exception to the exclusionary rule); Stone v. Powell, 428 U.S. 465 (1976) (holding that state prisoners cannot litigate claims based on the exclusionary rule in habeas corpus proceedings as long as they had a full and fair opportunity to litigate the claim in prior proceedings).

117. *See* Crawford v. Washington, 541 U.S. 36, 42–68 (2004) (reviewing historical evidence of the original meaning of the Sixth Amendment).

118. Blakely v. Washington, 542 U.S. 296, 302–08 (2004).

119. *See id.* at 306–08 (framing the issue as a choice between a "manipulable standard [and] *Apprendi's* bright-line rule"); *see also* Stephanos Bibas, *Judicial Fact-Finding and Sentence Enhancements in a World of Guilty Pleas*, 110 YALE L.J. 1097, 1102 (2001) ("[T]he Court has repeatedly recognized that legislatures have historically had broad latitude to define crimes and punishments.").

120. Apprendi v. New Jersey, 530 U.S. 466, 524 (2000) (O'Connor, J., dissenting).

121. *Blakely*, 524 U.S. at 323 (O'Connor, J., dissenting).

122. STRAUSS, *supra* note 44, at 17.

123. Berman, *supra* note 69, at 89.

124. Brennan, *Contemporary Ratification, supra* note 82, at 435.

125. District of Columbia v. Heller, 554 U.S. 570, 595 (2008) ("There seems to us no doubt, on the basis of both text and history, that the Second Amendment conferred an individual right to keep and bear arms.").

126. McDonald v. City of Chicago, 130 S. Ct. 3020, 3026 (2010) ("[W]e hold that the Second Amendment right is fully applicable to the States.").

127. *See Heller*, 554 U.S. at 573–618 (marshalling the historical evidence supporting an individual right to bear arms).

128. *See McDonald*, 130 S. Ct. at 3121–22 (Breyer, J., dissenting) (presenting the historical evidence disputing the *Heller* holding); *Heller*, 554 U.S. at 637–680 (Stevens, J., dissenting) (making the historical case against a strong individual right to bear arms).

129. *See Heller*, 554 U.S. at 595–600 (discounting the importance of the preamble); *id*. at 582–83, 593–95 (relying on English authority); *id*. at 612–19 (relying on evidence of the original understanding of the Second Amendment from the late 19th century).

130. *See* United States v. Lopez, 514 U.S. 549 (1995) (invalidating a federal statute prohibiting possession of a firearm in a school zone).

131. *See* Scalia, *supra* note 45, at 863 ("[T]he main danger in judicial interpretation of the Constitution... is that the judges will mistake their own predilections for the law.").

CHAPTER THREE

1. JOHN HART ELY, DEMOCRACY AND DISTRUST, at vii, 101–04 (1980).

2. Paul Brest, *The Substance of Process*, 42 OHIO ST. L.J. 131, 142 (1981).

3. *See* ELY, *supra* note 1, at vii ("Contemporary constitutional debate is dominated by a false dichotomy."); *id*. at 1 ("Today we are likely to call the contending sides 'interpretivism' and 'noninterpretivism.'").

4. *Id*. at 73.

5. *Id*.

6. *Id*. ("[T]he constitutional decisions of the Warren Court evidence a deep structure significantly different from the value-oriented approach favored by the academy.").

7. United States v. Carolene Prods. Co., 304 U.S. 144, 145–46, 152 n.4, 154 (1938).

8. ELY, *supra* note 1, at 87.

9. *Id.* at 102. In Ely's words, "life-tenured judges" simply are not "better reflectors of conventional values than elected representatives." *Id.* But at the same time, "elected representatives are the last persons we should trust" with identifying process failures. *Id.* at 103. Hence the need for appointed judges—who are "comparative outsiders" in our governmental system and "need worry about continuance in office only very obliquely"—to scrutinize the legislative process for market malfunctions. *Id.*

10. *Id.* at 92.

11. *Id.* at 99; *see also id.* (discussing the obsolescence of the Third Amendment).

12. *See id.* at 99 (citing the failure of the Prohibition movement as evidence that "attempts to freeze substantive values do not belong in a constitution"); *see also id.* at 98 (observing that while slavery was a protected value in the original Constitution, the Reconstruction Amendments enshrine "*non*slavery" as a value "single[d] out for protection now").

13. *Id.* at 102–03.

14. *Id.* at 103 ("Malfunction occurs when the *process* is undeserving of trust, when . . . the ins are choking off the channels of political change to ensure that they will stay in and the outs will stay out."); *see id.* at 111–12 (discussing First Amendment principles).

15. *Id.* at 134.

16. *See, e.g., id.* at 135 ("No matter how open the process, those with most of the votes are in a position to vote themselves advantages at the expense of the others, or otherwise to refuse to take their interests into account.").

17. *Id.* at 76 (quoting United States v. Carolene Prods. Co., 304 U.S. 144, 152 n.4 (1938)).

18. *Id.* at 153, 158–59.

19. *Id.* at 159 ("By seizing upon the positive myths about the groups to which they belong and the negative myths about those to which they don't, or for that matter the realities respecting some or most members of the two classes, legislators, like the rest of us, are likely to assume too readily that not many of 'them' will be unfairly deprived, nor many of 'us' unfairly benefited.").

20. *See id.* at 146–48 (defending the "tight fit" and "substantial weight" requirements of strict scrutiny).

21. *See infra* notes 69–77 and accompanying text (discussing Ely's applications of "representation-reinforcing" judicial review).

22. ELY, *supra* note 1, at 181 ("In saying that so clearly I have set myself up for a familiar form of attack: 'You'd limit courts to the correction of failures of representation and wouldn't let them second-guess the substantive merits? Why, that means you'd have to uphold a law that provided for _____!'").

23. *Id.* at 182 (arguing that some laws "couldn't conceivably pass").

24. *Id.* at 183 ("[C]onstitutional law appropriately exists for those situations where representative government cannot be trusted, not those where we know it can.").

25. *See Symposium in Honor of John Hart Ely,* 57 STAN. L. REV. 695 (2004); *Symposium on* Democracy and Distrust: *Ten Years Later,* 77 VA. L. REV. 631 (1991); Symposium, *Constitutional Adjudication and Democratic Theory,* 56 N.Y.U. L. REV. 259 (1981); Symposium, *Judicial Review Versus Democracy,* 42 OHIO ST. L.J. 1 (1981).

26. ELY, *supra* note 1, at 103.

27. *See* District of Columbia v. Heller, 554 U.S. 570, 573–610 (2008) (canvassing the historical debate over the meaning and scope of the Second Amendment).

28. *See* Roe v. Wade, 410 U.S. 113, 130–47 (1973) (discussing abortion practices from ancient Rome to 1970).

29. ELY, *supra* note 1, at 102.

30. U.S. CONST. amend. V ("No person shall...be deprived of life, liberty, or property, without due process of law....").

31. U.S. CONST. amend. XIV, § 1 ("[N]or shall any State deprive any person of life, liberty, or property, without due process of law....").

32. ELY, *supra* note 1, at 183.

33. *See supra* Chapter Two, notes 39–51 and accompanying text.

34. *See* William J. Brennan, Jr., *The Constitution of the United States: Contemporary Ratification,* 27 S. TEX. L. REV. 433, 438 (1986).

35. *See* ELY, *supra* note 1, at 73 (stating that the interpretivist-noninterpretivist debate "leave[s] us in a quandary" between losing out on the "evident spirit" of certain constitutional provisions and "constituting the Court a council of legislative revision").

36. *See infra* notes 40–83 and accompanying text.

37. 130 S. Ct. 3020 (2010) (incorporating the Second Amendment against the states).

38. ELY, *supra* note 1, at 72.

39. *Id.* at 87, 100, 102 n.*.

40. *Id.* at 103 ("A referee analogy is also not far off: the referee is to intervene only when one team is gaining unfair advantage, not because the 'wrong' team has scored.").

41. *Confirmation Hearing on the Nomination of John G. Roberts, Jr. to Be Chief Justice of the United States: Hearing Before the S. Comm. on the Judiciary*, 109th Cong. 55–56 (2005) (statement of John G. Roberts, Jr.) ("Judges are like umpires. Umpires don't make the rules, they apply them. The role of an umpire and a judge is critical. They make sure everybody plays by the rules, but it is a limited role. Nobody ever went to a ball game to see the umpire....I will remember that it's my job to call balls and strikes, and not to pitch or bat.").

42. *See* Brest, *supra* note 2, at 141–42.

43. *See id.* at 140 ("Physicists have their law of conservation of matter; economists have their law of no free lunch. The analogue in constitutional law may not yet have a name, but it amounts to the same thing: you can't get something out of nothing.").

44. *See* ELY, *supra* note 1, at 103, 131–34.

45. *See* U. S. Senate, Committee on Rules & Administration, Rules of the Senate XXII, Precedence of Motions, http://rules.senate.gov/public/index.cfm?p=RuleXXII.

46. *See, e.g.*, Sheldon Goldman et al., *Clinton's Judges: Summing Up the Legacy*, 84 JUDICATURE 228, 239 (2001) (describing Democratic Senators' complaints of anonymous "secret holds" on their judicial nominations).

47. *See* Elizabeth Garrett, *Term Limitations and the Myth of the Citizen-Legislator*, 81 CORNELL L. REV. 623, 638 (1996) (discussing Congress's heavy reliance on a seniority system for selecting "chairmen of committees and subcommittees").

48. ELY, *supra* note 1, at 103.

49. *See* Jane S. Schacter, *Ely and the Idea of Democracy*, 57 STAN. L. REV. 737, 738 (2004) (arguing that there are "significant ambiguities in the concept of democracy as Ely employed it").

50. U.S. CONST. art. III, § 1 ("The judicial Power of the United States, shall be vested in one supreme Court, and in such inferior Courts as the Congress may from time to time ordain and establish.").

51. *See* Colegrove v. Green, 328 U.S. 549, 556 (1946) (Opinion of Frankfurter, J.) ("Courts ought not to enter this political thicket. The remedy for

unfairness in districting is to secure State legislatures that will apportion properly, or to invoke the ample powers of Congress. The Constitution has many commands that are not enforceable by courts because they clearly fall outside the conditions and purposes that circumscribe judicial action.").

52. *See* Vieth v. Jubelirer, 541 U.S. 267 (2004) (5–4 opinion, with Justice Kennedy concurring only in the judgment, dismissing as nonjusticiable a challenge to Pennsylvania's allegedly partisan gerrymander).

53. Ely does not discuss "internal processes" in *Democracy and Distrust.* But internal process can pose just as much of a threat as external process to the values Ely seeks to protect. *Cf.* ELY, *supra* note, at 103 (describing the goals of process theory as preventing legislative majorities from "clogging the channels of change or...acting as accessories to majority tyranny").

54. *Id.* at 134 (quoting J. Skelly Wright, *Beyond Discretionary Justice*, 81 YALE L.J. 575, 585 (1972) (reviewing KENNETH CULP DAVIS, DISCRETIONARY JUSTICE: A PRELIMINARY INQUIRY (1969)).

55. *See* Whitman v. Am. Trucking Ass'ns, Inc., 531 U.S. 457, 474–75 (2001) (applying an "intelligible principle" standard for nondelegation while stating that "the degree of agency discretion that is acceptable varies according to the scope of the power congressionally conferred"); *see also* Douglas H. Ginsburg & Steven Menashi, *Nondelegation and the Unitary Executive*, 12 U. PA. J. CONST. L. 251, 258 (2010) ("Ongoing confrontation with the political branches appeared too perilous a course for the Court and, though it has never overruled *Schechter Poultry* or expressly repudiated the 'intelligible principle' standard of *J.W. Hampton*, its standards for intelligibility have become so flaccid that the Congress may now delegate authority to regulate the private sector in 'the public interest, convenience, or necessity' and to be 'generally fair and equitable.'").

56. *See* ELY, *supra* note 1, at 111–12 (discussing a process-based approach to the First Amendment).

57. Citizens United v. FEC, 130 S. Ct. 876, 887–88, 913 (2010).

58. McConnell v. FEC, 540 U.S. 93, 204–09 (2003).

59. 494 U.S. 652 (1990).

60. *Citizens United*, 130 S. Ct. at 886 (citing *Austin*, 494 U.S. 652).

61. *Id.* at 904 (quoting First Nat'l Bank of Boston v. Bellotti, 435 U.S. 765, 777 (1978)). While the Court declared *Hillary: The Movie* to be protected political speech, it upheld the portions of BCRA requiring

Citizens United to disclaim any affiliation with candidates and disclose the party "responsible for the content" of the advertisement. *Id.* at 913–16. In the Court's view, such requirements "help citizens make informed choices in the political marketplace." *Id.* at 914 (internal quotations and citations omitted).

62. ELY, *supra* note 1, at 111–12; *see also Citizens United*, 130 S. Ct. at 897 (describing how the provision of BCRA at issue prohibited corporations from engaging in certain forms of political discourse, such as "expressly advocat[ing] the election or defeat of candidates" or "broadcast[ing] electioneering communications within 30 days of a primary election and 60 days of a general election").

63. ELY, *supra* note 1, at 115 n.27.

64. Kathleen M. Sullivan & Pamela S. Karlan, *The Elysian Fields of the Law*, 57 STAN. L. REV. 695, 702 (2004) (internal quotation marks omitted).

65. *Citizens United*, 130 S. Ct. at 930 (Stevens, J., dissenting).

66. Sullivan & Karlan, *supra* note 64, at 701–02.

67. *Citizens United*, 130 S. Ct. at 947, 974 (Stevens, J., dissenting).

68. Ely barely talks about campaign finance reform in *Democracy and Distrust*; his discussion of the topic is cabined to one footnote about *Buckley v. Valeo. See* ELY, *supra* note 1, at 115 n.27; *see also* Buckley v. Valeo, 424 U.S. 1 (1976) (per curiam) (upholding limitations on individual contributions to political campaigns and provisions requiring parties to disclose the names of certain contributors, but invalidating limitations on expenditures by candidates). But even there, Ely does not discuss the substance of the case much. Instead, he simply criticizes the Court for applying a "markedly weak[]" balancing test to political speech. ELY, *supra* note 1, at 115 n.27.

69. *See* ELY, *supra* note 1, at 73, 101, 153, 177.

70. *Id.* at 155 ("Legislation on the basis of 'stereotype' . . . is the way legislation ordinarily proceeds, as in most cases it must.").

71. *Id.* at 159.

72. *Cf.* Brest, *supra* note 2, at 137–38 (noting the facility with which plaintiffs could transform rights claims into process claims).

73. *See* ELY, *supra* note 1, at 162.

74. *Id.* at 154, 159–61, 162–64, 166–69, 170–71.

75. Michael J. Klarman, *The Puzzling Resistance to Political Process Theory*, 77 VA. L. REV. 747, 787 (1991).

76. Samuel Issacharoff, *The Elusive Search for Constitutional Integrity: A Memorial for John Hart Ely*, 57 STAN. L. REV. 727, 730 (2004). Judge Bork has made a similar point:

> Ely's theory, which purports to take judges out of the business of making policy decisions, in fact plunges them into such decisions by requiring that they distinguish between cases in which groups lost in the legislative process for good reason (burglars) and those in which they lost for discreditable reasons (aliens, the poor, homosexuals, etc.). I fear that this is another point at which his system collapses. The results it produces turn out to be just another list of results on the liberal agenda which the Court must enact because legislatures won't.

ROBERT H. BORK, THE TEMPTING OF AMERICA 199 (1990). Bork later adds: "How does one know that a political market, which appears to be democratic, is nevertheless 'systematically malfunctioning'? I suspect one knows that because one dislikes the way the vote turned out." *Id.* at 197.

77. ELY, *supra* note 1, at 175, 176.

78. *See* 5 U.S.C. § 553(b) (requiring agencies to give public notice of proposed rulemakings); 5 U.S.C. § 553(c) (guaranteeing "interested persons" an "opportunity to participate" in rulemaking); 5 U.S.C. § 554(b) (requiring notice of, among other things, the time, place, nature, and legal basis for administrative hearings); 5 U.S.C. § 556 (establishing process requirements for administrative hearings); 5 U.S.C. § 702 (guaranteeing a right of review to any "person suffering legal wrong because of agency action, or adversely affected or aggrieved by agency action within the meaning of a relevant statute").

79. U.S. CONST. amend. XIV, § 1 ("[N]or shall any State deprive any person of life, liberty, or property, without due process of law....").

80. ELY, *supra*, at 103. Ely does not actually discuss how courts should approach separation of powers questions in *Democracy and Distrust*. The charitable reading of this omission is that Ely correctly recognizes that courts should be extremely chary of inserting themselves in such disputes. At the same time, however, Ely's observation that courts are "in a position objectively to assess claims" that "our elected representatives in fact are not representing the interests of those whom the system presupposes they

are" could easily be read as an open invitation—indeed a prescription—for courts to bring their "objective" perspective to bear on such conflicts. *Id.*

81. *Id.* at 102.

82. *Cf. id.* at 73 (arguing that a noninterpretivist approach "constitut[es] the Court a council of legislative revision").

83. 531 U.S. 98 (2000) (per curiam) (holding that standardless manual recounts of ballots cast in Florida in the 2000 presidential election violated the equal protection clause).

CHAPTER FOUR

1. Judge Posner's academic writings are impressive, both in content and sheer volume. In this discussion, I look primarily at his recent book *How Judges Think*. While it is intended more as a descriptive work about how judges actually decide cases than as a normative account of how they should decide them, *see* RICHARD A. POSNER, HOW JUDGES THINK 6 (2008) [hereinafter Posner, HOW JUDGES THINK]; its description of a pragmatic judge largely tracks Posner's normative descriptions of pragmatic judges in earlier works and is accompanied by a normative defense of pragmatic judging; *see id.* at 249–55.

2. *Id.* at 237, 251.

3. *See* Richard A. Posner, *The Role of the Judge in the Twenty-First Century*, 86 B.U. L. REV. 1049, 1066 (2006) [hereinafter Posner, *The Role of the Judge*].

4. Richard A. Posner, *Against Constitutional Theory*, 73 N.Y.U. L. REV. 1, 3 (1998) [hereinafter Posner, *Against Constitutional Theory*].

5. *See* Posner, *The Role of the Judge*, *supra* note 3, at 1051–52; *see also* Richard A. Posner, *Legal Reasoning from the Top Down and from the Bottom Up: The Question of Unenumerated Constitutional Rights*, 59 U. CHI. L. REV. 433, 445 (1992) ("Logic, science, statistical inquiry, the lessons of history, shared intuitions—none of these techniques of either exact or practical reasoning can slay them, or even wound them seriously in the eyes of those drawn to them for reasons of temperament or personal experience.") [hereinafter Posner, *Legal Reasoning from the Top Down and from the Bottom Up*].

6. Richard A. Posner, *The Supreme Court, 2004 Term—Foreword: A Political Court*, 119 HARV. L. REV. 31, 41 (2005) [hereinafter Posner,

A Political Court]; *see also* Richard A. Posner, *Constitutional Law from a Pragmatic Perspective*, 55 U. TORONTO L.J. 299, 300 (2005) (reviewing DAVID M. BEATTY, THE ULTIMATE RULE OF LAW (2004)) [hereinafter Posner, *Constitutional Law from a Pragmatic Perspective*].

7. Richard A. Posner, Response, *The State of Legal Scholarship Today: A Comment on Schlag*, 97 GEO. L.J. 845, 853 (2009) [hereinafter Posner, *The State of Legal Scholarship*].

8. POSNER, HOW JUDGES THINK, *supra* note 1, at 13.

9. Posner, *The State of Legal Scholarship*, *supra* note 7, at 853. Posner has criticized most of the current constitutional theories at length. *See, e.g.*, POSNER, HOW JUDGES THINK, *supra* note 1, at 324–42 (Justice Breyer's "active liberty" theory); Richard A. Posner, Democracy and Distrust *Revisited*, 77 VA. L. REV. 641 (1991) (political process theory); Richard A. Posner, *Bork and Beethoven*, 42 STAN. L. REV. 1365 (1990) (originalism).

10. Posner once argued that "legal reasoning worthy of the name inescapably involves the creation of theories to guide decision," but that such theories should be modest in scope. Posner, *Legal Reasoning from the Top Down and from the Bottom Up*, *supra* note 5, at 439, 446–47. Lately he resists using the word "theory" in describing his own pragmatism, acknowledging it is a "theory" in one sense but arguing it is better cast as skepticism about grand theorizing. *See* Posner, *Against Constitutional Theory*, *supra* note 4, at 9.

11. POSNER, HOW JUDGES THINK, *supra* note 1, at 87.

12. *See id.* at 13, 230–31.

13. *See, e.g.*, Richard A. Posner, Comment, *Pragmatism Versus Purposivism in First Amendment Analysis*, 54 STAN. L. REV. 737, 738–39 (2002) [hereinafter Posner, *Pragmatism Versus Purposivism in First Amendment Analysis*; Richard A. Posner, *Pragmatic Adjudication*, 18 CARDOZO L. REV. 1, 4 (1996) [hereinafter Posner, *Pragmatic Adjudication*].

14. POSNER, HOW JUDGES THINK, *supra* note 1, at 40.

15. *See id.* at 240–41; *see also* Posner, *Pragmatic Adjudication*, *supra* note 13, at 16.

16. *See* POSNER, HOW JUDGES THINK, *supra* note 1, at 80, 176–79.

17. *See, e.g., id.* at 239 ("[S]hortsighted pragmatists [are] blinded by the equities of the case to the long-term consequences of their decision; it is [for them that] the pejorative expression 'result oriented' should be reserved.").

18. Richard A. Posner, The Rise and Fall of Judicial Self-Restraint 29 (April 19, 2011) (unpublished manuscript) [hereinafter Posner, Judicial Self-Restraint].

19. *See* Posner, *A Political Court, supra* note 6, at 40–54 (arguing that the Supreme Court's constitutional decisions are largely unconstrained by legal materials).

20. *See* Posner, *Constitutional Law from a Pragmatic Perspective, supra* note 6, at 307–08.

21. *See id.* at 302, 306.

22. *Cf.* POSNER, HOW JUDGES THINK, *supra* note 1, at 264–65 (noting that it is an open question whether our judicial structure, which Posner argues makes pragmatic judging inescapable, is worth it).

23. *See* Posner, *Constitutional Law from a Pragmatic Perspective, supra* note 6, at 304 (noting that intensive fact-based adjudication is "rarely done, or doable"); *cf.* RICHARD A. POSNER, THE PROBLEMS OF JURISPRUDENCE 300 (1990) ("All too often, pragmatism without science is mush.") [hereinafter POSNER, THE PROBLEMS OF JURISPRUDENCE].

24. *See* POSNER, HOW JUDGES THINK, *supra* note, at 49. Interestingly, Judge Posner's votes very often coincide with his originalist colleague Judge Frank Easterbrook. *See* Jeffrey S. Sutton, *A Review of Richard A. Posner,* How Judges Think, 108 MICH. L. REV. 859, 866 (2010) (noting that the two voted together in 98.9% of cases between 1985 and 1999, a 1.6% higher rate than that for Seventh Circuit judges generally).

25. POSNER, HOW JUDGES THINK, *supra* note 1, at 249, 254–55.

26. *See id.* at 249–50 (suggesting that Clinton v. Jones, 520 U.S. 681 (1997), was unpragmatic but not "wrong").

27. *Id.* at 241. Because of Posner's skepticism about moral and political argumentation, he thinks such a consensus will come about through common backgrounds, experiences, and temperaments rather than reasoned collaboration. *See generally* RICHARD A. POSNER, THE PROBLEMATICS OF MORAL AND LEGAL THEORY (1999) [hereinafter POSNER, THE PROBLEMATICS OF MORAL AND LEGAL THEORY].

28. *See* POSNER, HOW JUDGES THINK, *supra* note 1, at 249.

29. *See, e.g., id.* at 105–17; Posner, *Pragmatism Versus Purposivism in First Amendment Analysis, supra,* at 744 (acknowledging that some costs may be more salient than others, potentially distorting the pragmatic analysis).

30. *See, e.g.*, Frank H. Easterbrook, *Pragmatism's Role in Interpretation*, 31 HARV. J.L. & PUB. POL'Y 901, 901–02 (2008) ("The case for pragmatism is easy to state. Our Constitution is old, and modern society faces questions that did not occur to those who lived during the Civil War and penned the reconstruction amendments, let alone those who survived the Revolutionary War and wrote the Constitution of 1787.").

31. Kennedy v. Mendoza-Martinez, 372 U.S. 144, 160 (1963); *see also* Terminiello v. Chicago, 337 U.S. 1, 37 (1949) (Jackson, J., dissenting) ("There is danger that, if the Court does not temper its doctrinaire logic with a little practical wisdom, it will convert the constitutional Bill of Rights into a suicide pact.").

32. 545 U.S. 677, 698 (Breyer, J., concurring in the judgment). That is, Posner rightly praises Justice Breyer's willingness to temper his otherwise strong views about the limits created by the establishment clause by considering the disastrous consequences of such a strict rule. Whether those strong views about the establishment clause are correct in the first instance is a different question.

33. Posner, *A Political Court, supra* note 6, at 100.

34. POSNER, HOW JUDGES THINK, *supra* note 1, at 246; *see also* Allen v. Wright, 468 U.S. 737, 751 (1984) (prudential standing); United Pub. Workers v. Mitchell, 330 U.S. 75, 89–90 (1947) (ripeness).

35. *See, e.g.*, Colo. River Water Conservation Dist. v. United States, 424 U.S. 800 (1976); R.R. Comm'n v. Pullman Co., 312 U.S. 496 (1941); Burford v. Sun Oil Co., 319 U.S. 315 (1943).

36. *See, e.g.*, Safford Unified Sch. Dist. No. 1 v. Redding, 129 S. Ct. 2633, 2639 (2009).

37. *See, e.g.*, Mathews v. Eldridge, 424 U.S. 319 (1976).

38. *See, e.g.*, POSNER, HOW JUDGES THINK, *supra* note 1, at 118–21.

39. *See, e.g.*, Posner, *A Political Court, supra* note 6, at 76–78.

40. *See infra* text accompanying notes 66–70.

41. *See* POSNER, HOW JUDGES THINK, *supra* note 1, at 19–56 (reviewing social science literature on judging).

42. *Id.* at 256–63.

43. *See* Frank B. Cross, *What Do Judges Want?*, 87 TEX. L. REV. 183, 200–02 (2008) (reviewing POSNER, HOW JUDGES THINK, *supra* note 1).

44. *Cf.* John F. Manning, *Statutory Pragmatism and Constitutional Structure*, 120 HARV. L. REV. 1161, 1170–71 (2007).

45. Richard Fallon forcefully argues that by leaving the door open to well-intentioned judicial deception, pragmatism violates norms of judicial candor grounded in the rule of law. *See* Richard H. Fallon, Jr., *How to Choose a Constitutional Theory*, 87 CAL. L. REV. 535, 573–74 (1999). Any argument that pragmatism or discussions of pragmatism will increase candor in judicial decisionmaking thus needs to be qualified by the possibility that pragmatism could also increase judicial sleight of hand.

46. *See supra* text accompanying notes 16–23.

47. *See* POSNER, HOW JUDGES THINK, *supra* note, at 44–45.

48. *See, e.g.*, Posner, *Pragmatism Versus Purposivism in First Amendment Analysis*, *supra* note 13, at 740 ("[T]hat pragmatism doesn't necessarily imply balancing at retail and that any such case-by-case balancing is proper only outside the settled core of doctrine . . . are particularly important [points] to bear in mind in order to prevent a too-quick collapse of pragmatism into case-by-case balancing.").

49. *See* Posner, *A Political Court*, *supra* note 6, at 52.

50. *See* POSNER, HOW JUDGES THINK, *supra* note 1, at 237.

51. *See, e.g.*, Planned Parenthood of S.E. Pa. v. Casey, 505 U.S. 833 (1992); Citizens United v. FEC, 130 S. Ct. 876 (2010).

52. *See* POSNER, HOW JUDGES THINK, *supra* note 1, at 86–87.

53. Posner, *The Role of the Judge*, *supra* note 3, at 1062.

54. *See, e.g.*, POSNER, HOW JUDGES THINK, *supra* note 1, at 84.

55. *Cf.* Nancy Leong, *The* Saucier *Qualified Immunity Experiment: An Empirical Analysis*, 36 PEPP. L. REV. 667 (2009) (suggesting cognitive dissonance leads courts doing qualified immunity analysis to avoid finding both a constitutional violation and that the right at issue was not clearly established).

56. Posner, *Pragmatic Adjudication*, *supra* note 13, at 4.

57. *Id.* at 16; *cf.* Posner, *Pragmatism Versus Purposivism in First Amendment Analysis*, *supra* note 13, at 751 (discussing widespread consensus on issues such as child pornography).

58. Roe v. Wade, 410 U.S. 113 (1973).

59. POSNER, HOW JUDGES THINK, *supra* note 1, at 242–43.

60. Jeffrey Rosen, *Overcoming Posner*, 105 YALE L.J. 581, 596 (1995) (reviewing RICHARD A. POSNER, OVERCOMING LAW (1995)) (discussing pragmatism's impracticality because of the institutional deficiencies of courts).

61. Patricia M. Wald, *Some Observations on the Use of Legislative History in the* 1981 *Supreme Court Term*, 68 Iowa L. Rev. 195, 214 (1983) (quoting author's conversation with Judge Harold Leventhal) (internal quotation marks omitted).

62. *See* sources cited *supra* note 57.

63. J. Mark Ramseyer, *Not-So-Ordinary Judges in Ordinary Courts: Teaching* Jordan v. Duff & Phelps, Inc., 120 Harv. L. Rev. 1199, 1209 (2007).

64. *See* David Cole, *The Poverty of Posner's Pragmatism: Balancing Away Liberty After 9/11*, 59 Stan. L. Rev. 1735, 1737–43 (2007) (reviewing Richard A. Posner, Not a Suicide Pact: The Constitution in a Time of National Emergency (2006)).

65. *See* Cass R. Sunstein, *Cost-Benefit Analysis Without Analyzing Costs or Benefits: Reasonable Accommodation, Balancing, and Stigmatic Harms*, 74 U. Chi. L. Rev. 1895, 1902–05 (2007).

66. *See* Michael Sullivan & Daniel J. Solove, *Can Pragmatism Be Radical? Richard Posner and Legal Pragmatism*, 113 Yale L.J. 687 (2003) (reviewing Richard A. Posner, Law, Pragmatism, and Democracy (2003)) (criticizing Posner's failure to embrace the radical potential of pragmatism) [hereinafter Posner, Law, Pragmatism, and Democracy].

67. Posner, How Judges Think, *supra* note 1, at 118, 119.

68. Rosen, *supra* note 60, at 596.

69. *See, e.g.*, Thomas O. McGarity, *A Cost-Benefit State*, 50 Admin. L. Rev. 7, 12–16 (1998) (noting that risk assessment and cost-benefit analysis are inevitably partial, uncertain, and dependent on contestable assumptions); Wendy E. Wagner, *The Science Charade in Toxic Risk Regulation*, 95 Colum. L. Rev. 1613, 1628–50 (1995) (arguing that agencies engage in conscious and unconscious "science charades").

70. *See, e.g.*, Williamson v. Lee Optical, Inc., 348 U.S. 483 (1955) (upholding a statute requiring a prescription to fit lenses and to duplicate or replace them).

71. Manning, *supra* note 44, at 1170. Although Manning's discussion takes place in the statutory interpretation context, it is equally applicable to the constitutional one. Pragmatists must view judges as striking out on their own in crafting constitutional law rather than simply as agents of the Framers or ratifiers.

72. United States v. Marshall, 908 F.2d 1312, 1335 (7th Cir. 1990) (en banc) (Posner, J., dissenting), *quoted in* Manning, *supra* note 44, at 1166.

73. *See* Manning, *supra* note 44, at 1169–70 (citing POSNER, LAW, PRAGMATISM, AND DEMOCRACY, *supra* note 66, at 70–71).

74. *Cf.* Posner, *A Political Court, supra* note 6, at 54 (noting that a Justice could "accept . . . wholeheartedly" the political nature of constitutional law and vote in cases just as a legislator would).

75. *See, e.g., id.* at 102 ("If the Supreme Court is inescapably a political court when it is deciding constitutional cases, let it at least be restrained in the exercise of its power, recognizing the subjective character, the insecure foundations, of its constitutional jurisprudence."); Richard A. Posner, *Justice Breyer Throws Down the Gauntlet,* 115 YALE L.J. 1699, 1705 (2006) (reviewing STEPHEN BREYER, ACTIVE LIBERTY: INTERPRETING OUR DEMOCRATIC CONSTITUTION (2005)) ("I am old fashioned in regarding the invalidation of a federal statute as a momentous step that should not be taken unless the unconstitutionality of the statute is clear. . . .").

76. POSNER, HOW JUDGES THINK, *supra* note 1, at 246–47. Of course, minimalist decisions have some drawbacks. They can increase decision and error costs, and they often provide inadequate guidance to lower courts. *See* Neil S. Siegel, *A Theory in Search of a Court, and Itself: Judicial Minimalism at the Supreme Court Bar,* 103 MICH. L. REV. 1951, 2005–09 (2005).

77. Manning, *supra* note 44, at 1170 (quoting POSNER, LAW, PRAGMATISM, AND DEMOCRACY, *supra* note, at 71) (first alteration in original).

78. Sullivan & Solove, *supra* note 66, at 694 (quoting POSNER, LAW, PRAGMATISM, AND DEMOCRACY, *supra* note 66, at 60); *see also* Posner, *Pragmatic Adjudication, supra* note 13, at 4.

79. Posner, *A Political Court, supra* note 6, at 98.

80. *See* Posner, *Pragmatic Adjudication, supra* note 13, at 4.

81. *Cf.* Daniel A. Farber, *Shocking the Conscience: Pragmatism, Moral Reasoning, and the Judiciary,* 16 CONST. COMMENT. 675, 686 (1999) (reviewing POSNER, THE PROBLEMATICS OF MORAL AND LEGAL THEORY, *supra* note) 27 ("[C]ontinuity with the past is not simply a prejudice; it is a way of maintaining and redefining national identity.").

82. Posner, *Pragmatic Adjudication, supra* note 13, at 16.

83. Eric Rakowski, *Posner's Pragmatism*, 104 HARV. L. REV. 1681, 1682 (1991) (reviewing POSNER, THE PROBLEMS OF JURISPRUDENCE, *supra* note 23) (internal citations omitted).

84. Posner, *Pragmatic Adjudication, supra* note 13, at 14.

85. POSNER, HOW JUDGES THINK, *supra* note 1, at 249.

86. *See, e.g.*, ROBERT H. BORK, THE TEMPTING OF AMERICA 165–66 (1990) (recognizing originalism's limits).

87. Posner, *Against Constitutional Theory, supra* note 4, at 9.

88. Cass R. Sunstein, *The Minimalist Constitution, in* THE CONSTITUTION IN 2020, at 37, 37 (Jack M. Balkin & Reva B. Siegel eds., 2009) [hereinafter Sunstein, *The Minimalist Constitution*].

89. CASS R. SUNSTEIN, ONE CASE AT A TIME: JUDICIAL MINIMALISM ON THE SUPREME COURT 3 (1999) [hereinafter SUNSTEIN, ONE CASE AT A TIME].

90. Sunstein, *The Minimalist Constitution, supra* note 88, at 41.

91. Posner, *Against Constitutional Theory, supra* note 4, at 9.

92. SUNSTEIN, ONE CASE AT A TIME, *supra* note 89, at ix–x ("Alert to the problem of unanticipated consequences, [minimalism] sees itself as part of a system of democratic deliberation; it attempts to promote the democratic ideals of participation, deliberation, and responsiveness. It allows continued space for democratic reflection from Congress and the states. It wants to accommodate new judgments about facts and values.").

93. Sunstein, *The Minimalist Constitution, supra* note 88, at 42.

94. SUNSTEIN, ONE CASE AT A TIME, *supra* note 89, at x.

95. Cass R. Sunstein, *The Supreme Court, 2007 Term—Comment: Second Amendment Minimalism:* Heller *as* Griswold, 122 HARV. L. REV. 246, 267 (2008) [hereinafter Sunstein, *Second Amendment Minimalism*].

96. Posner, *Against Constitutional Theory, supra* note 4, at 9.

97. Sunstein, *Second Amendment Minimalism, supra* note 95, at 270–71.

98. SUNSTEIN, ONE CASE AT A TIME, *supra* note 89, at x.

99. Posner, *Judicial Self-Restraint, supra* note 18, at 16.

100. Posner, *Against Constitutional Theory, supra* note 4, at 9.

101. POSNER, THE PROBLEMATICS OF MORAL AND LEGAL THEORY, *supra* note 27, at 154, 242.

102. POSNER, HOW JUDGES THINK, *supra* note 1, at 255.

103. Richard A. Posner, *Past-Dependency, Pragmatism, and Critique of History in Adjudication and Legal Scholarship*, 67 U. CHI. L. REV. 573, 596 (2000).

104. *See* POSNER, HOW JUDGES THINK, *supra* note 1, at 264–65.

105. Richard A. Posner, *1997 Oliver Wendell Holmes Lectures—The Problematics of Moral and Legal Theory*, 111 HARV. L. REV. 1637, 1681 (1998).

106. Posner, *Legal Reasoning from the Top Down and from the Bottom Up*, *supra* note 5, at 447 (citing PHILIPPA STRUM, LOUIS D. BRANDEIS: JUSTICE FOR THE PEOPLE 361 (1984) ("[Justice Brandeis] told [his law clerks] that Justice Holmes employed a simple rule of thumb for judging the constitutionality of statutes, summed up in Holmes's question, 'Does it make you puke?'" (alterations in original)); *see also, e.g.*, Posner, *A Political Court*, *supra* note 6, at 54–55.

107. Posner, *Legal Reasoning from the Top Down and from the Bottom Up*, *supra* note 5, at 447.

108. 381 U.S. 479 (1965).

109. Posner, *Legal Reasoning from the Top Down and from the Bottom Up*, *supra* note 5, at 448–49.

110. Posner, *Pragmatic Adjudication*, *supra* note 13, at 11–12.

111. Steven D. Smith, *The Pursuit of Pragmatism*, 100 YALE L.J. 409, 449 (1990).

CHAPTER FIVE

1. James B. Thayer, *The Origin and Scope of the American Doctrine of Constitutional Law*, 7 HARV. L. REV. 129, 135 (1893).

2. Furman v. Georgia, 408 U.S. 238, 418 (1972) (Powell, J., dissenting); *see also* New State Ice Co. v. Liebmann, 285 U.S. 262, 311 (1932) (Brandeis, J., dissenting) (recognizing that "we must be ever on our guard, lest we erect our prejudices into legal principles").

3. *Speech of Learned Hand on "I Am an American Day" (May 21, 1944)*, in THE SPIRIT OF LIBERTY: PAPERS AND ADDRESSES OF LEARNED HAND 189, 190 (Irving Dillard ed., 3d ed. 1960).

4. Gregg v. Georgia, 428 U.S. 153, 176 (1976) (plurality).

5. Barry Friedman, *The Birth of an Academic Obsession: The History of the Countermajoritarian Difficulty, Part Five*, 112 YALE L.J. 153, 254 (2002) (quoting Eugene V. Rostow, *The Supreme Court and the People's Will*, 33 NOTRE DAME L. REV. 573, 575 (1958)).

6. Griswold v. Connecticut, 381 U.S. 479, 530–31 (1965) (Stewart, J., dissenting).

7. HAND, *supra* note 3, at 189–90.

8. Thayer, *supra* note 1, at 142, 152.

9. A.L.A. Schechter Poultry Corp. v. United States, 295 U.S. 495 (1935).

10. *See, e.g.*, Carter v. Carter Coal Co., 298 U.S. 238 (1936) (Hughes, C.J., joined by Cardozo, Brandeis, and Stone, JJ., dissenting).

11. See Minersville Sch. Dist. v. Gobitis, 310 U.S. 586 (1940), *overruled by* W. Va. State Bd. of Educ. v. Barnette, 319 U.S. 624 (1943).

12. See Miranda v. Arizona, 384 U.S. 436, 504 (1966) (Harlan, J., dissenting); Reynolds v. Sims, 377 U.S. 533, 589 (1964) (Harlan, J., dissenting).

13. *See, e.g.*, Griswold v. Connecticut, 381 U.S. 479, 499 (1965) (Harlan, J., concurring).

14. United States v. Morrison, 529 U.S. 598 (2000); United States v. Lopez, 514 U.S. 549 (1995).

15. Kimel v. Fla. Bd. of Regents, 528 U.S. 62 (2000); City of Boerne v. Flores, 521 U.S. 507 (1997).

16. Duncan v. Louisiana, 391 U.S. 145, 178 (1968) (Harlan, J., dissenting); *see also id.* at 176 ("Apart from the approach taken by the absolute incorporationists, I can see only one method of analysis that has any internal logic. That is to start with the words 'liberty' and 'due process of law' and attempt to define them in a way that accords with American traditions and our system of government.").

17. Brandeis, for example, remained vigilant to the dangers of "bigness." *See, e.g.*, Erie R.R. Co. v. Tompkins, 304 U.S. 64, 78–79 (1938) (requiring courts to conduct a choice of law analysis in diversity cases, rather than relying on federal general common law). Powell, on the other hand, sought to prevent the general mandate of the equal protection clause from eviscerating the tradition of local control of local schools. *See, e.g.*, San Antonio Indep. Sch. Dist. v. Rodriguez, 411 U.S. 1, 42–43 (1973) (upholding school funding system allowing districts to supplement state aid with tax on property within their jurisdiction).

18. Jeffrey Rosen, *Why Brandeis Matters*, THE NEW REPUBLIC, July 22, 2010, at 25.

19. 347 U.S. 483 (1954).

20. 372 U.S. 335 (1963).

21. 377 U.S. 533 (1964).
22. 384 U.S. 436 (1966).
23. *See* Kelo v. City of New London, 545 U.S. 469 (2005).
24. *See* Penn Central Transp. Co. v. New York City, 438 U.S. 104 (1978).
25. *See* District of Columbia v. Heller, 554 U.S. 570 (2008).
26. *See*, e.g., San Antonio Indep. Sch. Dist. v. Rodriguez, 411 U.S. 1, 70–71 (1973) (Marshall, J., dissenting) (arguing that Texas's property-tax-based system of school funding should be struck down for violating the equal protection clause and the infringing on "the right of every American to an equal start in life"); Dandridge v. Williams, 397 U.S. 471, 508 (1970) (Marshall, J., dissenting) (contending that Maryland's decision to impose a cap on the total amount of aid for needy families unconstitutionally discriminates against larger families).
27. 410 U.S. 113 (1973).
28. 402 U.S. 1 (1971).
29. 553 U.S. 723 (2008).
30. *Cf.* Keyes v. Sch. Dist. No. 1, 413 U.S. 189, 246 (1973) (Powell, J., concurring in part and dissenting in part):

> Neighborhood school systems, neutrally administered, reflect the deeply felt desire of citizens for a sense of community in their public education. Public schools have been a traditional source of strength to our Nation, and that strength may derive in part from the identification of many schools with the personal features of the surrounding neighborhood.... Many citizens sense today a decline in the intimacy of our institutions—home, church, and school—which has caused a concomitant decline in the unity and communal spirit of our people. I pass no judgment on this viewpoint, but I do believe that this Court should be wary of compelling in the name of constitutional law what may seem to many a dissolution in the traditional, more personal fabric of their public schools.

31. *See, e.g.*, Military Commissions Act of 2006, Pub. L. No. 109–366, 120 Stat. 2600 (codified in scattered sections of 10, 18, 28, and 42 U.S.C.).
32. *Compare* McDonald v. City of Chicago, 130 S. Ct. 3020, 3114–16 (2010) (Stevens, J., dissenting), District of Columbia v. Heller, 554 U.S. 570, 679–80 (2008) (Stevens, J., dissenting), Parents Involved in Cmty. Sch. v. Seattle Sch. Dist. No. 1, 551 U.S. 701, 848–49 (2007) (Breyer, J.,

dissenting), *and* United States v. Lopez, 514 U.S. 549, 604 (1995) (Souter, J., dissenting), *with* Lawrence v. Texas, 539 U.S. 558, 603–04 (2003) (Scalia, J., dissenting), Stenberg v. Carhart, 530 U.S. 914, 980 (2000) (Thomas, J., dissenting), *and* Planned Parenthood of S.E. Pa. v. Casey, 505 U.S. 833, 1002 (1992) (Scalia, J., concurring in part and dissenting in part).

33. LEARNED HAND, THE BILL OF RIGHTS 73–74 (1958).

34. *Cf.* William J. Brennan, Jr., *The Constitution of the United States: Contemporary Ratification*, 27 S. TEX. L. REV. 433, 440 (1986) ("As government acts ever more deeply upon those areas of our lives once marked 'private,' there is an even greater need to see that individual rights are not curtailed or cheapened....").

35. *See* BARRY CUSHMAN, RETHINKING THE NEW DEAL COURT 3 (1998) (describing the traditional perception that Justices Van Devanter, McReynolds, Sutherland, and Butler voted together in opposition to New Deal legislation).

36. Stuart Taylor Jr., *Why the Justices Play Politics*, WASH. POST, July 14, 2010, at A19.

Acknowledgments

. . .

No one writes a book without a good deal of help. My longtime friends Judge Karen LeCraft Henderson of the District of Columbia Circuit Court of Appeals and Professor Laurens Walker of the University of Virginia Law School encouraged me to undertake this project and, more importantly, insisted I keep at it.

It's best to seek help where you can expect to receive pushback, and I have not been disappointed. Spirited debate and lively correspondence with Professor Geoffrey Stone of the University of Chicago Law School have been of inestimable assistance. As the editor of the Inalienable Rights series, Geof never misses a hole in an argument. Every author should have a sparring partner like Geof—he makes the act of writing challenging and fun.

Professor Michael Seidman of Georgetown University Law Center made a number of excellent suggestions, large and small. Geof clerked for Justice Brennan and Mike for Justice Marshall during the time I clerked for Justice Powell. Perhaps our bosses would be pleased that our friendships have survived the years.

Judge Richard Posner of the Seventh Circuit Court of Appeals was most generous with his time and criticism. His insights were all the more welcome because of the disagreements between us set forth herein.

I have dedicated this book to all my law clerks who have made service in the federal judiciary such a personal and professional delight. Four in particular have helped with this book—Jeffrey Johnson, Rakesh Kilaru, Mark Little, and Brian Schmalzbach.

My thanks go also to the good people at Oxford University Press. It has been a real pleasure to work with them. Thanks especially to Dave McBride, whose campaign against legal jargon and sense of just the right place to put a thought have made this a better book.

Finally, my dearest Lossie, our children, Nelson and Porter, and even our grandson, Harvie, have had to put up with more than they should have during the writing of this book. I know authors often say this, but alas, in my case it's true.

Index

...